I Wonder ...

The Science of Imagination

J.D. Rhodes

Clink
Street

London | New York

Published by Clink Street Publishing 2017

Copyright © 2017

First edition.

ISBN: 978-1-911525-35-6 paperback
978-1-911525-36-3 ebook

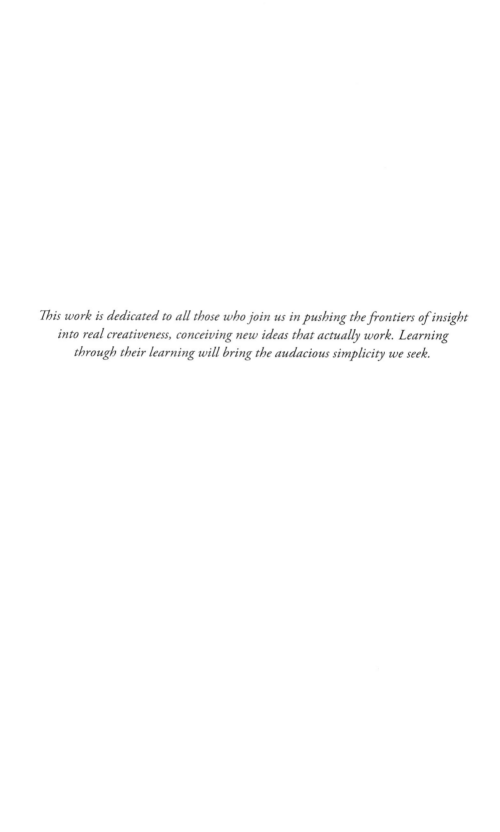

This work is dedicated to all those who join us in pushing the frontiers of insight into real creativeness, conceiving new ideas that actually work. Learning through their learning will bring the audacious simplicity we seek.

Also by Jerry Rhodes

The Colours of Your Mind
Conceptual Toolmaking

Contents

Preface

This book is for readers with aspiration, and there are three main themes:

1. to persuade everyone that imagination matters, and why
2. to encourage, by connecting with the natural and spontaneous workings of mind
3. to show how to use those thinking muscles that try to reach the new and unusual

It is vital to be clear that the exercise of imagination does not assure creativity, but simply opens up the potential for a creative concept, action, product or output. New is not always good, just as being different does not make something 'creative'. The more unusual a new idea (which therefore feels brilliant) the more you will need the development of real information and the scrutiny and confirmation of Judgement. This makes recourse to imagination a strategic choice, driven either by desperation or aspiration for the exceptional. It raises the very level of thought.

A strategic driver of imagination is the assault on almost every one of the normal or conventional thinking tactics. Know it or not, you will be subverting how things normally work in your mind or else entirely outreaching them. Small wonder that imagination is unpopular with most ordinary people who turn thumbs down on anything seen as outlandish. It is outlandish.

Here I focus on imagination, one of the tripod of great forces of thought that work so well because of their mutual opposition. *Imagination* goes outside conventional perceptions to find something unusual, and so has a strong need for the *information* that shows its idea is feasible and which of course must submit finally to *judgement:* will the idea work and do I like it? How could wise decisions be made without thinking up further objectives, options and risks than the merely obvious? Imagination comes up with new possibilities and raises one's confidence that we haven't missed out vital information or contributions to judgment.

Successful creativity comes when you can separate these three, use each one to help the others and thus optimise the living tensions between them. An idea can claim to become 'creative' only when it is shown to work exceptionally well.

Foreword

Could there possibly be a 'science' of imagination? If the title evokes surprise or disbelief in you, then you are among those most likely to enjoy being led into its secrets by this book where you will find in the Contents the skeleton of what is meant by the 'science' of imagination. Each chapter begins with its summary.

The word 'science' comes from the Latin *Scientia,* for knowledge, understanding and methodology, and embraces what we normally consider to be the arts as well as science. Science and art are simply two differing but mutually supportive approaches to the same aim, to discover the outstanding.

The science we know demands clear disciplines of rational thought so as to assure that real life observations are used to reach conclusions that are sound and bullet-proof. This can never be abandoned – but the trick is to know when to delay judgment until after you have thought further than what is known. To be certain, we impose limits on our mind that might not be valid, so it is vital to envision what lies the other side of the moon, even when you cannot see. Good scientists know that 'real science' is greater than what the layman understands about it. Your sense of wonder invites you to explore beyond, outside and within what normally counts for knowledge and understanding. It allows you to think what <u>might </u>become true which cannot be observed yet.

High risk means high returns or gain. What is so special and exciting about imagination is the freedom it gives to take risk – but without risk. Awareness of its potential danger both puts you on your mettle and summons up the real information needed for judgment before taking action. So more opportunities may be envisioned that could never be reached by ordinary thought.

The action research underpinning this book comes from years of work with businesses keen on practical ways to raise their performance. But uncovering what lies beneath and behind our thought process applies everywhere, and in universities is named 'the philosophy of science'. I am, therefore I think. Everything anyone does is due to what they think. There is a real and urgent need to know how and why we think what we think, especially in light of the conflicting aims of logic and imagination. Every politician who refuses to wonder 'what might happen if' is doomed to the oncoming disaster.

Many people, even schools, have warm feelings about being 'creative or imaginative' without knowing much of what either means. Attempts at wild imagination at the wrong moment could be even worse than insisting on being rigidly rational too soon. The 'science' entails first being able to recognise the kind of thinking to deal with the situation facing you; second, where you are most likely to put in the wrong kind of effort; and third how best to bring the full powers of logic and imagination to bear when the time is right. This recognition is made easier by using the same language for all three of these aspects of thought. This book offers a rationale and a methodology for expanding the use of your mental resources to embrace more possibilities than you normally allow, so as to reach exceptional ideas. It draws on running our leading-edge training programmes with many thousands of able and experienced managers.

Rational thought is essential, but by no means sufficient, especially in a world where everything around us is changing faster and faster. Thought is the engineering of knowledge and experience to achieve a better result than we would without it. Past experience no longer solves the new situations we keep facing, which need us to embrace and integrate the extra dimension of imagination. The bonus is that this 'wonder' makes the rest of your brain work better, too. Now the impossible comes sooner.

Building on a career spent innovating as a manager inside business, I founded my own consulting practice with a mission to bring more creativity to work. I have spent half a lifetime exploring how successful people think when facing challenging situations, so as to determine what makes for success that can be spread further. From the start, I focused especially on how exceptional ideas seemed to come when adopting methods of thought that were outside and beyond normal 'critical thinking' that we learn at school and university. The trouble is, once the powers-that-be have done their best to discourage or even destroy the creative instincts we were born with, the disciplines of the business world follow through and finish the job. That leaves all too many otherwise capable people reduced to thinking mainly in the most obvious ways.

My early work in this area caught the attention of Philips, Eindhoven, who invited me to join a team they had set up to research 'skilful thinking' and make this part of their management education around the world. Since then, I have developed the entire system known as Effective Intelligence, which is spread through my network of associates to leading companies, whose contribution to the research has been vital.

For me, what matters is to share more widely what we have discovered about reaching creative solutions, hoping to show that 'wonder' is more approachable than some people believe; indeed that everyone can learn how to make much more use of their own imagination, not leaving it to those possessing some mysterious arts. To reach out further round the world I have launched http://www.thunkies.com which is a new website, adding to the long-established http://www.effectiveintelligence.com.

I Wonder ...

The Science of Imagination

I
Why wonder?

Chapter 1
Imagination Matters

No one can do without wonder, and it should not be so rare, for it enhances all the rest of your mind. Better still, it offers access to exceptional achievement and escape from the impossible. Wondering allows and brings to you the universe of what has never been known or thought: what can only be imagined. Though many do not make the most of it, this gift belongs to everyone, to keep ahead of robots, ballooning knowledge and accelerating change. New approaches can be reached that would otherwise be out of bounds. Not only does wonder fuel vision and aspiration, it is the secret of learning things new, and makes whole all your other thinking processes. No one can do without imagination.

Why wonder?
1. "It's only your imagination"

Who would wish to be a sad soul without imagination, living on a flat earth, in a life missing the third dimension? Yet to challenge the ordinary, demands the courage of leadership as well as a special kind of questioning. The way to begin is to become aware of your powers of imagery. This is the special language that heightens your perceptions beyond normal sensory experience and whose richness brings infinite opportunity for new ideas to form. Then you can take your mind over with all manner of positive assaults, in search of changes that will surprise. Open up to wonder, and allow yourself to hear your imagination: intuition to be listened to. The seemingly impossible may be realized because you have found a solution that transcends your experience up to now. Everyone is able to do this, but it takes skill. Practicing this will give the insight that a challenging situation needs thinking that goes beyond the obvious in various ways. If you are someone who never makes a decision that you then kick yourself for, read no further—or raise your sights a bit higher! This book is for those who aspire to greater things by exploiting more fully the gift of wonder.

I wonder… How would you like to capture something before you actually know it? This is the skill of imagination, of creating a reality that is not yet there. If you fail to grab any short cuts to speeding things up by inspired guessing, you are condemned to rely entirely on what you know already, what has happened. Who needs to be so stuck in the mud and backward-thinking? You'd certainly risk being wrong, but your speculation *could* turn out to be true. So we all need deeper insight into what we are doing in our heads when we wonder, and into how else we must think, to ensure the risk pays off well.

Whenever things don't turn out well, it is often because "Oh, I didn't think of that!" You are not likely to if you don't even try to think outside your tiny box. Few of us were deliberately taught how to think—we learned unofficially, through a life of thousands of experiences. Few of us have arrived at any comprehensive whole. Your brain reacts to stimulus, especially that from surprise. Surprise results from something being different from the proven, which is usually what you know and believe already, and how normal, critical thinking would wish to keep you safe. So allow yourself to wonder, to seek what is not yet known, for the scope is as vast as the universe. Because thinking cannot work without imagination, this book invites you to look further than you normally see and so reach beyond the stars.

"Every child is an artist: the problem is how to remain an artist when he grows up."
PABLO PICASSO

All too soon after he has been put to bed, Johnny appears at the door of the sitting room.
"What is it, darling?" says his mother. "Why aren't you asleep?"
"'Cos there's a pirate under my bed, and he has this cutlass, and if I get too close, he'll cut me off at the knees."
After a cup of warm cocoa and a little hugging, his father takes him upstairs again. "It's all right, Johnny," he tells him. "It's only your imagination."

Of course Johnny's parents mean well, but what a thing to say! 'Only,' indeed—notice how pejorative was his comforting, as if only reality matters. As bad as restricting your child to crawling and walking, never allowing him to run or leap. The word 'imagination' is wrongly bracketed with fantasy, delusions, wild goose chases, invalid conclusions, unreliable evidence, perhaps even something untrustworthy.

It gets worse. Without imagination, you cannot hope or fear, suggest or avoid. There is no aspiration or opportunity, no resourceful ingenuity, because you have no way of dealing with the unknown future, stuck with the opinions and facts you already have. You are not allowed to suppose, or speculate about what might have happened or what might have caused it. The result is, even rational logic is crippled: no chance to think up anything new or original. We would remain in a mental stone age.

There are people who feel that imagination ought to remain fuzzy or a mystery. But most want practical ways to bring it into play and raise their chances of generating new ideas. This often entails optimizing the conflict between wild imagination and normal thought. So this book sets out to simplify the creation of unusual insight, exploring the amazing variety of imaging and hoping to offer a glimpse into the ineffable universe of mind.

Figure 1.1 Wondering (after Cecil William Rhodes)

2. Who on earth can do without imagination?

No one can do without imagination, which should not be seen as something rare. It enhances all the rest of your mind and offers access to exceptional achievement and escape from the impossible. It is for Everyman, and it was Marilyn Monroe who declared, "*You can learn to use more of the 100% talent you've got.*"

Imagination enables us to see what is not actually existing, for what you do not know and cannot find out can <u>only</u> be imagined. To do a better thing altogether: what might that be? Aspiration brings inspiration, vision for the future.

Just consider: which is the larger, what we already hold in our experience, or what may be outside that sphere? No contest. The experience that's inside our mind is only a fraction of what we don't know; that's outside. Moreover, the paradox is that the more that is learned, the smaller that fraction becomes, not larger, because every extra piece of learning spawns multiple applications and connections with other knowledge. This is how strategic it is, and how it is strategic. It is imagination that brings IN to our experience what has until now been OUTside it. Think what we 'know' to be true yet we are mistaken; what we do (not) believe in, but we are wrong; what we only imagine, that would have worked out, but we rejected it. It helps to learn what we do not know or believe <u>yet</u>.

> *I am on the operating table and the surgeon's scalpel slips, severing all connections between imagination and the rest of my mind.*

What a scenario! I would have to give up conceiving anything exceptional, for now I could do only the obvious, see only what is there, and not what might be. All I could say would be prosaic, pedestrian, boring. I'd always be vulnerable, being unable to think of any kind of threat to my safety until it happened. Even my wishes would be limited to what I already know, so any aspiration for something better is out of my ken. Anything difficult or not before met is bound to defeat me, for I'll never think of any other way of dealing with the issue, let alone a way out. So blinkered would I be that I would accept without question what others propose and act with the rigid obedience of a robot.

As for seeing a situation with the eyes of someone else, such empathy is beyond me, not because I am unkind but because I am not me. Everything feels inevitable. But worst of all I'd be unable to learn anything that is not explicitly shown to me. That is all I could take in. The notion of using an experience for anything other than its immediate function or purpose is totally out of bounds. There is no future, because it hasn't happened yet, but maybe I won't care, because my spirit of curiosity is dead. And as the witless man said dolefully, "I may be dumb but I'm also slow."

"Why didn't they think of that?" you exclaim in despair—but we can all be guilty. Without imagination, expect performance to be mediocre at best and a disaster when the task is difficult and success-critical. You will remain stuck with your best reasoning about existing knowledge if you allow no space for wondering. But if you don't know and cannot judge, what else is there but to use your imagination? It is the only source to draw on that takes you out of a hole or reaches further than you can normally grasp.

Yet my work in business and industry has revealed that being creative is seen by most as some kind of 'also-ran'; indeed the government refers to a very narrow arty sector as 'creative industries.' They are clearly blind to the fact that always thinking how to do something better is essential to any company's survival and prosperity. Imaging is like a fluid that runs through and into and between and out of all kinds of your thinking. Aims and values, opportunities, solutions to problems, winning support, recognizing potential threats to success, ways to reduce risk, social effectiveness and making competition irrelevant are just a few obvious needs. In fact, every time we think up any kind of idea, this is what we are using. So the rightful role of imagination is extremely significant, and every single reader should play it. We all know the frustration felt when rational efforts have failed and our goal seems impossible; when what we want is not worth the cost or we just don't have the resources; when a bad compromise is unavoidable or we need something unique or special. Actually, to know when <u>not</u> to use our ingenuity is the secret.

To wonder is to go beyond what we 'know' to be right or true, so it gives you the edge, especially when ignored by all the others! It is now clear that imagination is the ingredient essential for learning, even the wit to recognize someone else's idea. Just as the progress of civilization has exponentially developed the ratio of gain to cost, imagination does the same to the rest of your mental faculties. Unlike the grinding machinery of logic, so often deliberate and step by step, imagination is allowed to make great swoops. It's extremely fast and, in the form of intuition, it seems like magic.

3. What imagination is for

For me, a main function is to give more scope for the exercise of free will. We all do things we would never have done if only we had thought of something that revealed how stupid they were. Likewise, we fail to do what proves to be really essential and we are always shooting ourselves in the foot.

"*What scientists are interested in is the pursuit of ignorance*" (Stuart Firestein, TED talk, September 2013). Knowledge generates an awareness of ignorance, just as "*every answer begets more questions*" (Kant) so the result is ignorance of higher quality!

Everyone confronting a 'wicked' problem knows that the quality of his ideas will be more effective than brute force. S/he looks for ways to avoid the zero-sum game, where a gain in one aspect must mean losing out somewhere else in the pie chart. Sometimes the real enemy is not your apparent opponent but the dreaded third party called Waste. Be sure to look beyond and in between the lines, so as to defeat Murphy's Law. Spotting something special or surprising about the situation in hand can make the impossible easy. How to think wide enough to reach the idea to exploit this vital chink should be worth exploring in the chapters that follow.

Imagination is always needed for anything especially difficult, yet people usually ignore it, and look what happens—it fails to be achieved. Many failures are down to not having thought up a better solution. Without insight gained from wondering, every action would be taken blind. "Damn! I never thought of that!" Conversely, it brings the gift of surprise, putting you ahead of others if they have ignored wondering. Unless you challenge the merely obvious solutions, better ones don't even get a chance. Invention has two faces: conceiving the need and coming up with the solution that fulfills it.

More often than we realize, we should go around reason, so as not to be frustrated by knowledge that is not yet available. We should hope to make unusual connections that might be relevant and to reach a view of the future that is <u>more than</u> an extrapolation of the past. Openness to ideas is useful, for example, when:

- Rational or logical attempts so far have failed
- It seems impossible
- Resources seem to be needed which are unavailable
- There is a premium on uniqueness, or competitive edge
- Conflict of interests would otherwise lead to unsatisfactory compromise
- Any gain costs far too much
- How something works or why it went wrong is baffling—you cannot 'see' it.

At latest estimate, we know of only 4.9% of the matter in the universe, of which 27% is dark matter and 68% dark energy. This is only a scintilla of what there is to be imagined, so there's plenty of scope elsewhere! Using normal thinking, we are unlikely to discover much that is unusual, so it's a must to exploit the twin concepts of 'nottery' and 'else,' each more than mere fact. Nottery is a playful word to capture the idea of anything that would be expectable, but is surprisingly not so. "*That's not what I meant!*" is at the core of so many misunderstood instructions, specifications, rules and laws. Things can be significant by their absence as much as by their presence. *The clue for Sherlock Holmes in* The Hound of the Baskervilles *was that the dog did <u>not</u> bark in the night* when he normally would have done. The critical secret to high quality work is what is <u>not</u> done, how <u>little</u> material is needed for a bridge to remain standing. You pay the high quality consultant or expert not for what he does but for what he doesn't (need to) do.

4. Imaging is for all, for Everyman

"He has a strong sense of wonder"
HIS MOTHER,
ON STEPHEN HAWKING

Imagination has been called our most precious human characteristic. Creativity is for much else than inventing products: we need better and different processes and methodologies; ways of living, how to get the best out of other people, and, not least, ways to get the most out of oneself! We all start with the wonderful skill of 'making things up' and most of us could develop our innate talents so as to live up to our potential. Some are born more creative than most, and others die less creative than when they were young. Sadly, education causes too many to actively shut out those 'instincts,' or throw a wet blanket over the sparks. How about actually doing more unusual things, and doing things unusually?

Man is a creative animal: everyone you know reveals glimpses of this. Yet creativity is too often regarded as the province of exceptional people, special professional occupations or particular events. Beyond its obvious validity, this notion is misleading and not much help to the rest of us. It is actually a barrier to progress when imagination is thought to be restricted to the arts, design, literature and poetry, music and dance, breakthroughs in science and mathematics, or Nobel Prize discoveries. Such iconic examples can make an artificial fence, excluding a thousand others by mistake.

It is in the hundreds of day-to-day situations that assail us all that creativity counts most. And what is brilliant or elusive for one person might be obvious to another, especially at another time or place. **So it's useful to see 'creativeness' in the <u>approach</u> of the person concerned, rather than simply in the unique originality of any idea itself.** What can even mentally disabled children teach us? There are creative skills, which can be learned and taught. By studying what a champion is doing when he hits the ball so effortlessly, others can be coached to improve their game. Even the champions do this too. We can develop our muscles even of imagination, simply through guidance on how to flex them, and then through exercise. A wonderful box of tools doesn't make a craftsman—until he puts them to use, and then they start improving him, as well as his output. Everyone can produce exceptional results by being resourceful in unusual ways with whatever they have. *Look what Robinson Crusoe did.* You can change what you think about and how you think about it. The skills are there to be used by anyone, especially when you let a bit of 'natural you' escape.

5. You can't help using imagination

Actually, you can't help using imagination. Whatever you are doing, pictures are constantly forming in your head. Just being alive entails receiving a constant stream of impressions jostling together in a moving kaleidoscope, to form some image in your mind. When what is happening close to you evokes no response at all, makes no impression, has no effect, it's a sign of being deaf or blind, or dead. Normal thinking is unlikely to discover much that is unusual, but surprise keeps us on our toes, a rescue from mediocrity or failure. How we kick ourselves when we didn't think of something or when we didn't think someone would hear a different meaning in what we said.

Whenever you take on something of which you have no experience, to wonder is your only hope. Luckily we are hardwired with 'thinking-instincts' of a kind. Some of these, like curiosity, specialize in imagination—otherwise how could infants and children learn so fast? Children are good at making things up. Learning, imagination and emotion are the sources and drivers of what even the youngest child will do, without any guidance. Indeed when he becomes more 'civilized' he loses some of his natural skills and propensities. They become swamped by the chosen and planned thinking practices for bringing his imagination and emotions under control so as to function effectively, proactively and reliably. In the child those very 'thinking-intentions' (they are not technically instincts) exist before his thought has been developed from experience and without being taught to do things better.

6. So why do people ignore it?

A challenging situation demands an extra-ordinary attitude, yet by definition this will be new or extreme, even outlandish, so will need strength of mind to overcome the opposition it is bound to stir up.

We do know from my research with nearing 150,000 individuals that imagination is the least preferred thinking stance. It's hard to swim outside the shoal of course, but your habits come both from what you're born with and from the customs and attitudes encouraged (or discouraged!) by parents, education, work and society in general. The power of No is more immediate and greater than Yes or Maybe. Undue modesty or diffidence also plays a part.

The image of thinking as requiring too much time is all too common, not all due to Rodin's famous statue! Creative thought is seen as even worse. Actually this is mistaken belief, for thinking is far faster, cheaper and much less risky than doing, making or building something. Indeed, imagination takes huge short cuts to its hopefully exceptional conclusion. Reason so often requires one to construct a logical path, step by step, down from one peak to the valley and up the other side to the succeeding peak, so that one's route provides the audit trail. Imagination, like emotion, has no need to grind the machinery of logic. The spider spins his own thread to reach wherever he will across space. *Like a bird, an image in your skull needs no firm pathway up the cliff, but can take you in huge swoops through space and violent contractions in time, putting things together in an entirely new way.* If experience of reality is often the stimulus for thought, your emotion is often the driver, and imagination the leader.

It shouldn't nowadays be too hard to build a case for 'going far out,' except that many people are stupid! To start with, Change is unavoidable. John

Maynard Keynes, the great economist, once remarked, "When the facts change, I change my mind. What do you do, sir?" You can treat life as a broad river on which we are embarked, so that we are always moving with the flow. If a person remains locked into his status quo, determined not to change, then he stands solid as a rock, thus actually creating turbulence in the quiet river. So to remain the same in a changing world entails either failure in what you have been doing, or success in some different field. Either way, it's change. So the log that <u>moves</u> in the bosom of the stream causes the <u>least turbulence</u>.

7. Raising the bar—aspiring to higher standards
"If anything is certain, it can't be any good" said an award winning architect, the liveliness of whose work was still in evidence at the age of 97 when interviewed by the BBC recently.

Generally, people recognize four or five kinds of situation where they need to think beyond the obvious. First, however badly they actually do it, everyone can do what they see as a brainstorm. Next favorite is in the envisioning of goals, forming a picture of where you would really wish to be, or what you might achieve. Third, thinking up all the criteria that matter for a good design is clearly something left undone, else there would not be so many badly designed products—and nor would so many people actually buy these! Fourth is the energy put into predicting risks and threats: all governments seem to be the champions of the Law of Unintended Consequences—but too late! Finally, leaders need a special power of imagination to look ahead strategically, to recognize and form patterns in world events, patterns that others might not spot so readily. If they are business leaders, it will give their organization competitive advantage. If they are leaders of a nation, this is what their nation expects of them.

Miele, that robust manufacturer of washing machines and a pillar of the German Mittelstand, has a motto: *immer besser*—forever better. Like 'continuous improvement' and 'think better: do better' it embodies the idea of innovation. Luckily, doing better things better results in becoming a better person. "The harder I practice, the luckier I get," as the great golfer Gary Player remarked. It may be a rare gift to envision some goal or event or reality which no one has ever even glimpsed, and is perhaps why people feel "I cannot do imagination." But as Churchill memorably observed: "We should always look farther than we can see." The first step is to believe you can, the second to keep widening your vision.

Civilization has developed the ratio of gain to cost out of all proportion, and this is what imagination does to the rest of your mental faculties: intuition works like magic. In fact, wonder helps us form the questions that initiate thought, realize beyond what we know, describe beyond what we experience, judge with criteria beyond our normal habit patterns of meaning. Of course, any form of thinking is faster than actually doing the action physically in the real world; it costs little and carries small risk unless or until you choose to act on it.

Imagination is the ingredient essential for learning, and nowadays every single person is on multiple learning curves. Innovations are coming in accelerated waves to break upon the shores of the developed world. Learning brings the difference between giving a starving man a fish and teaching him how to fish. Think what it did for the caveman once he conceived of a log to roll, a lever to lift a mountain, bow and arrows to kill the mammoth. "Give a man a fire and you warm him for a day: set him on fire and he will be warm for life!" '(Terry Prachett).

"Is there anything you can think of, that hasn't been invented yet?"
ERIC ASHBY, NATURALIST, TO HIS MOTHER WHEN HE WAS 10

That's aspiration!

Chapter 2
The Leadership of Original Thought

To think beyond the ordinary requires the leadership of questioning and the will to take on risk. Seeing the possible before all the others lends huge advantage, and it is unpopular only because anything strange or unfamiliar stirs up fear: whatever is new must by definition differ from what is already known or 'right', making it somehow 'wrong'. Yet if normal approaches to a problem are disappointing, it is surely worth seeking something new? Innovation would not happen without the imagination to think up questions and possibilities that do not exist. Difficult work is for leaders and demands unlikely questioning, not just routine stuff. This comes from imagination.

Leadership is often an aspiration but it takes many forms, from inspiration through getting people to agree with you, to the art of original thought. When you lead with a novel idea, others may not follow you, for their intellectual and emotional immune system rejects any alien substance as a dangerous intrusion. 'Never do anything for the first time' says the notice above the desk of the bureaucrat in Paris. Exceptional, original ideas require an approach that is different from the way we normally use our intelligence so that we reach things not-yet realized. Others will resist, making any innovation difficult, unless you can harness their exploring mind of curiosity.

Leaders tackle work that is difficult or challenging: that is thinking work. Creating a question from scratch entails a kind of imaging, both of the kind of answer you would hope for and also even of the kind of hook that might capture it. There is a world of difference between the questions that arise from these three situations.

What might be?

What should be?   What is?

Questions bring alive <u>the space between</u> these three positions: what causes this gap and how could we close it?

We saw that imagination is needed whenever you think and is especially active in the arrival and formation of a thought. It has to be key to inventiveness, discovery and all forms of learning. Anything new comes out of connections made that have been previously ignored because they are highly improbable, dissimilar and remote. As knee-jerk reactions usually attack anything unusual, great leadership is vital because you are doing something <u>before</u> anyone else. When either your ambition is high or you are at the bottom of a pit, the only thing for it is a new idea. You are the conscious taker of conceptual risk and Steve Jobs of Apple fame declared, "Innovation distinguishes a leader from a follower." Not everyone seeks to be a leader—some prefer to keep the score, rather than make the runs.

Creative innovation is a sign of life: as soon as one stops learning beyond experience, death is stealing over us. Invention not only opens up ways to progress but also brings renewal of our very selves. The big jumps come when you apprehend what is not yet known. Words such as *all, every, only* and *never*, often used without thinking, restrict opportunities and cut off anything else. The tragedy is that what we then miss might be the best solution.

The issue is this: thought is seen to be the connector between Input from observed experience and its Output or conclusion. But experience cannot be the sole source of our Input, because it has to have happened, to be real in the outside world. So a significant share of our Input is not 'real,' based on what we know of the world outside, but comes from our imagination, inside the head.

Financial investors are divided into two groups: those who know they don't know how their shares will perform and those who don't know they don't know. Ideally, people learn how to learn, perhaps the highest potential outcome of education. It is not very widespread yet, because in schools imagination is still suppressed rather than deployed and encouraged. The problem is that many truly great works of art or science have indeed been so original and different that they have made a shocking impact at first, and even been jeered at and shunned.

Innovation entails thinking up a better thing or doing better what already exists. Exceptional, original ideas require a different use of our intelligence. Only a few people (and this we can measure) have the magic skill to see the different, further applications of anything they experience, and this multiplies its value.

Figure 2.1. Leader on horseback

"What will painting do when I'm dead? It will have to walk over my body. There's no way round" (Picasso, age 19 in 1901). Truly advanced scientists are light-years ahead of the bovine UK government demand in 2009 that any science they would fund would need to be evidence-based! This echoed the attitude of a local government officer observed on a TV program: *You are not allowed to try out experiments unless or until you can be sure what the results will be.* How sound he felt he was! As Niels Bohr said in Essays 1932-57, *"If you are not profoundly shocked by the phenomena of quantum mechanics, then you haven't understood it."*

What of the role of imagination in art and in science? Most people think of art and science as entirely different domains of thought. But it is actually what they have in common rather than what separates them that really matters. For example, when anyone receives an insight, s/he may experience a flash of surprise recognition of unity, transcending familiar boundaries in a kind of 'beauty.' I believe a mathematician can feel this same soaring arc of elation. It is akin to the moment when you manage to simplify massive complexity into a single idea. Archimedes leapt from his bath into the public street, shouting "Eureka!" Those few 'lucky' ones who do this often are said to have flair, genius, star quality. As Napoleon told his generals, "Give me commanders in the field who are lucky." Those who often make something out of nothing we might call Imagineers and there is something of the outsider in every entrepreneur of the mind.

Thought is led by 'inventors' of various kinds. The Research & Development function of Philips, with whom I have worked as a consultant for about 30 years, involved around 16,000 people, some devoted to discovering new concepts in science and the majority developing new high-tech products. In part of the research I did for them, I involved a select few of their outstanding inventors. One conclusion we reached was that the most stunning insights come from the fusion of reason and imagination at white heat. The image created in this way is the 'product' that is extruded or that springs out of the space between. We will see later how two of our inner thinking-intentions, recognizing what distinguishes one group of phenomena from others, and making otherwise wildly irrational connections, cannot both live within pure Reason. Yet the invention of something original that can be made material so that it works is often the result of the collision of the rational and the supra-rational: a stroke of genius or divine energy.

Science then can justify the Imagineer abandoning normal laws, boundaries and properties so that impossible connections and conclusions can be reached. Of course, things feel incredible when we do not yet know enough—this is why we need to real-ize, to bring a new notion into reality. Before the physics was known, phenomena such as magnetism or any force field working at a distance were very puzzling; *surely heavy things fall faster? Why does this little cork float towards the edge of the bowl? How can holography be real? And why do waves and particles become each other?* Before we got inside the atom, how could we have known that the rules of sub-atomic physics might be as strange as quarks or charm?

It's amazing that two hundred and fifty years prior to Leonardo da Vinci, Roger Bacon, the 13th century Franciscan friar, predicted the airplane, submarine and telescope. What of the huge strides taken since 1660 by those giants in Oxford and London who founded the Royal Society? How did India come up with such advanced mathematics a thousand years ago? Over a millennium earlier, how did the Greeks conceive their geometry and the philosophical insights that still resonate today? To say nothing of ancient Egypt and China, far away! The great scientist is just as likely to take advantage of knowledge not justified by reasoning and intelligence, which is a way of describing intuition. In fact imagination has as great a role in science as in art—*Leonardo saw them as two aspects or halves of the same thing*.

1. Teaching is leading people to learn

Innovation requires first invention and then the education of the supporters and the market it needs. Kuan Tzu in 500 BC advised: "to score 1, sow a seed; to score 10, plant a tree; to score 100, educate the people." The Greek word '*ideon*,' from which 'idea' comes, means to see: "Now I see" means I understand suddenly what was not clear before—learning something new or anew.

Images are the heralds and harbingers of thought: it's through the gift of metaphor that thoughts come and so is how excellent teachers set about reaching them—and teaching them. Mahatma Gandhi exhorted, "Be the change you want to see in the world." Analogy was defined in Dr. Johnson's dictionary as a device that "brings together a use to which it cannot be put" and so is how to 'get the point' and recognize more unusual applications.

Imagination is not necessarily Creativity. American children are encouraged to believe that *Whatever can be imagined, can be achieved,* whilst the current fashion is to act as if doing something different or differently is a claim to 'creativity.' We see the awful results all round us, for it is all too easy to come up with something different—that doesn't work! For example the producers, and approvers, of millions of print graphics need to go back to some principles of communication, for these are being flouted in the interest of surprise, daring or just being unconventional. Because something <u>can</u> be done does not mean it <u>should be</u>. So some look askance at imagination, accusing a child of 'making things up' when they suspect a lie. Yet making things up is the closest you get to 'creating' out of nothing. Shakespeare spoke of seeing 'in the mind's eye' to convey what it's like to conceive something before it is there, without it being there, or at least without enough evidence for it. Creativity is associated with actions that pluck victory from disaster, success from the apparently impossible. Unusual thoughts steal a march on the majority, put a twist on the established order of things, and make fools of those who are informed only by sound probability.

What we 'know' is a fraction of what is possible—the whole of reality. Science rightly falls back on claiming probability, rather than truth, for which its search is continual. *When we can see inside a black hole, it might overturn many of our theories, including those of greats such as Einstein.* Most of what is true is still <u>not</u> known; most of what is believed is <u>not</u> certain; logical reasoning is <u>not</u> entire and complete and is not always the best route to something new or different. Of course it is sound to evaluate a new idea <u>after</u> reaching it. Despite this, in academic and even some (inadequate) scientific education, too much weight is given to existing knowledge and reasoned judgment; too little to going outside those limitations. Of course new conclusions must be 'evidence-based,' but it is ridiculous that learned papers can even be judged by the number of references per page! Does this cause trained minds to be averse to anything new? Surely it is not the real eye but the mind's eye that offers leadership of thought. So-called 'critical thinking' is too often restricted to followership of the thoughts and quotations of others.

2. Imagination takes risks

A leader is the conscious taker of conceptual risk. This works best when you separate <u>what</u> the idea will deliver from <u>how likely</u> it is to deliver it, for *as in a lottery, the bigger the prize, the less likely you will win!* An idea can be so subtle, fragile, ephemeral even, that it may die before it is allowed to materialize. He who hesitates is lost, so at least bring the fish on deck before deciding whether or not it's worth landing.

It is natural to think of vision and leadership in the same breath. In fact, vision often comes when imagination and emotion come together in one powerful surge, and that person becomes leader. The word 'visionary' is used for leadership both in thought and in motivation. The emotional force of belief drives not only for goals but also for ideas and options. Apart from its literal optical sense, vision describes a kind of revelation. Becoming inspired is so different from, yet akin to, inspiring others that we use the same word: vision. Margaret Thatcher was strong on inspiring through values but less so on new revelation. Alexander the Great, Caesar, Joan of Arc, Oliver Cromwell, Napoleon, Nelson and Shackleton all spring instantly to mind; probably more readily than Socrates, Pythagoras, Michelangelo, Shakespeare, Descartes, Coleridge, Mozart or Einstein. Scientists, philosophers, artistic geniuses, poets, musicians and writers may actually be greater movers and shakers of the world than the leaders of countries or military might. The difference is that the latter produced action, while the former did more for the invisible and underlying reasons for it. All were leaders, and it is arguable that those who lead the universe of thought have greater and more lasting impact than those who lead the physical world. The pen really can be mightier than the sword.

The majority of people do not take risks, and the things they do are humdrum: they are in the middle of the 'bell curve,' the normal distribution identified by the great mathematician Dr. Gauss. *Fishes in a shoal keep moving from the outside to the inside; as in a herd, there is safety in numbers.* By definition, the obvious comes first to mind, and it's typically felt to be safe that way. So, although originality is often at a premium, to be any different can feel risky. Yet perhaps this is not always a sensible survival strategy.

Figure A shows how confidence differs from probability. You have far more confidence in a probability of 0.2 than one of 0.5, where doubt is at its height.

Figure B shows that the middle ground of normality of ideas only feels safe: it is actually the area of maximum competition. This may justify going to the extremes of the unusual, where a niche market is more likely. Of course the unusual might prove either brilliant or a disaster. A sound evaluation system, especially if withheld until after exploration, makes it possible to go further out on a limb for competitive advantage.

Figure 2.2. Uncertainty bell curves

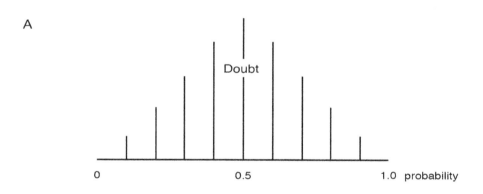

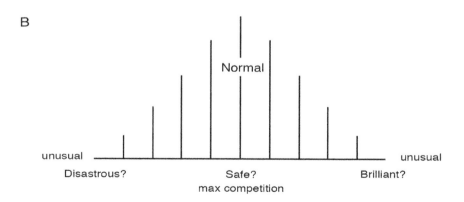

Most extreme ideas that succeed have faced being turned down over and over by many people, at first. J K Rowling is a recent example, yet she is long past 350 million copies of her books about Harry Potter. It's everywhere: works of art, the greatest operas and other musical works, extraordinary inventions such as the telephone, the computer and the cell phone, a long and wide-ranging catalogue of ideas that were at first rejected spans our history from the Greeks through the amazing Middle Ages, to the explosion of science and industry in the last few hundred years. More still, it seems the better the idea, the more advanced it was, the more likely it has been rejected by the majority who dwell in the middle of the herd, or bell curve! No surprise then that successful creativeness demands courage and persistence; more than just the first spark of an original concept.

3. Thought is led by questioning

Where do questions come from? Answers clearly come from knowledge and reasoning, but about what? I believe that they come from a universal and eternal system or process that shows us the questions most likely to produce the answers needed by the situation we are facing up to. But we don't always tap into this wisdom. For example, when reaching a decision, you just have to ask for the criteria which will reflect what matters to you when thinking up possible options; you have to ask what are the options or solutions beyond the obvious ones; you must find out what is known about the results that matter to you which each option is likely to deliver; and you're a fool if you don't question the risk of each solution. Taking risk further, when you wonder about effects that you fear as consequences of what you are about to do, and how serious they might be, you are straight into imagination. The same is true when you try to measure how likely it is that something would cause your plan to go wrong, and again when you think how that could happen. In short, it seems that all thought is born of questions we feel need answering, because it matters that we don't know enough. But to get exceptional answers, you might need exceptional, unusual questions.

Difficult work is thinking work: "I do, therefore I think." Good interpersonal behavior may avoid failure but does not of itself assure success, unless what you choose to do is right, and that needs thought. Skillful questioning brings leadership and the successful question may well be the most unlikely. I often have to assess the capability of people I barely know, and one way is to judge him or her by the questions they raise—or fail to raise. It is not just *what* you conclude, but also *how* you raise questions, especially unusual ones, for beneath or behind every thought is an (unspoken) question. In "The Fisher King," the man did not ask the question which would have cured the king of his condition of useless legs, because he had been told not to ask stupid questions about things he knew nothing about. Expert witnesses at a court of law can be disappointed with the quality of their own evidence, because they are allowed only to give answers to the questions raised by the barrister—but he may fail to deliver the question needed. Before you engage in a costly court case, test him or her by the quality of their questioning! If you don't know where you are going, any road will take you there, just as if you don't know what you seek, any answer satisfies your question.

4. Pure conceptual questions

Imagination is brought into play when exploring beyond what is known and/ or to find what is needed to come to a judgment: anything we seek outside experience calls for questions. But these can be of different kinds. You ask a question to find out what is known (facts). Or to be influenced by what or how someone else thinks (opinions). Or to open up into speculations as to what might possibly be conceived (suggestions). Unless deployed for advocacy, rhetoric or teaching purposes, the answers can be utterly unknown to the questioner. The only truth about the future comes from robust and well-established laws, for example of mathematics, physics or logic. We can predict with certainty that the apple will fall, that scaffolding based on 3, 4, 5, will be at proper right-angles and that the radius of any circle will predict its circumference at 3.14159, etc. Other questions can be used without any knowledge, confident they will deliver something relevant and useful. For instance, to ask *"What matters to you?"* will get at someone's values, what drives her personal judgment, why she will do something. *"What have you noticed?"* will tell you about his experience of reality. *"What could go wrong?"* produces a range of possibilities that might cause failure unless you do something. Such 'conceptual drivers,' each of a different nature, form the data base of a skill, as distinct from knowledge.

Questioning is challenging, testing, vital, demanding, senior, important, critical. In fact, whenever one has to read a document, article or serious book, a well-known trick is to form some questions you need answered by the piece.

This focuses your mind and makes the key information jump out of the page at you. The same is true when taking part in a meeting or listening to a discussion of any kind; in an interview, both parties should work with the questions each needs to be met, and also how to explore their answers to see if they have been satisfied, and what else remains.

Imagination is the faculty essential for bringing into the mind things of which one had low awareness, for instance, ways to challenge, enhance, change, expand, pursue curiosity, make unusual (dis)connections, allow intuition and generally go beyond the obvious. We use it to think up possible causes of a disaster—or the possible murderer in a crime novel. In the fields of art and aesthetics, it is imagination that 'separates the men from the boys' because it enriches your observation far beyond anything actually experienced. But these are only its most easily noticed roles. So conceiving an unrecognized need for improving our society and its interactions is as 'creative' as conceiving an idea that will help. It also puts you ahead of the game.

Luckily, there is a wealth of imagineering questions which can offer a high degree of confidence that they will provoke an unusual idea: "How could this be changed?" "Does it have to be like this always?" "Why is it so difficult?" "What would be surprising, but effective?" "How else might it be?" "Isn't there another way?" and so on.

"Science is what you do when you don't know what you are doing"

AT CERN, 2008, WHEN THE PARTICLE ACCELERATOR
EXPERIMENT HAD JUST BROKEN DOWN

5. A wide and deep search function

Your mind is like a parachute: it functions only when open—except you must know how and when to close it (down). Imagination is your widest-ranging and deepest search function. Even to uncover your own innermost thoughts and feelings, such as the basic reasons for doing something or not, is much harder than we at first think. What really are my emotions and values and wishes? So often, we find out only after the catastrophe. Per contra, when a trial unexpectedly turns up trumps, taking advantage quickly enough needs turbo-charged ingenuity, or you lose the lead it offers.

6. Seize the power of initiative

It is the questions <u>not</u> asked, that should have been, which account for the flaws in our thinking that so badly affect the outcome: <u>not trying to</u> think widely about something amounts to a crime against imagination. As Cardinal Richelieu observed in the 17th century (my paraphrase), *there is nothing so invisibly powerful as prudence, because it imagines what has not actually happened and takes action to prevent it or reduce its effects, so that no one ever realizes what has been done. Prudence is the art of a hero unsung.* Perhaps too many people consider that having to ask a question will betray their ignorance, so they will lose face. Even though to stop learning means decline, there are people who do not like to be considered a Learner. Others rejoice and seize the high ground.

"It is I who ask ze questions," as the classic foreign police chief is supposed to sneer to the spy he has captured. BBC journalists from Radio 4's flagship political program, "Today," when interviewing an important public figure should be alert to the phenomenon that just raising it lends a question the power of an answer, without any apparent responsibility for its effects. A kind of reality has been created that might have no truth in it. Being on the receiving end of a question often feels like being under attack or assault, facing an arrow with a real shaft behind it. So a really skillful questioner, such as Nicky Campbell or Shelagh Fogarty formerly on Radio 5 Live, may disguise a few questions within some other form, lest their 'victim' close down the hatches or even turn to attack.

As in the design of a scientific experiment, all questions contain within or beyond them the (hypothetical) seed of the answer. Some answers have no value, whether intentionally or not, and equally some questions deserve no response. There are of course tactical questions raised to test someone, to accuse or to put someone down, or to teach and to persuade. Some, concocted by clever lawyers or journalists in the tradition of the ancient Pharisees, put a question whose answer will condemn the responder, whatever he says, including his maintaining silence or refusing to answer. Politicians often fall prey to such smart tactics, instead of turning them back on the journalist. Both question and answer demand much ingenuity and there is a difference between not choosing to answer and choosing not to.

Creative and logical questioning also are not the same: you may use the former as trial stimuli and turn to others if one doesn't work; whereas logical questions must be asked and demand disciplined response. Creative questions try to uncover that insight into the incompleteness of our knowledge that has not yielded to logic and might solve our problem. I usually switch between the two if one is failing to deliver what I need.

Raising unusual questions is the business of philosophy—in fact I remember A J Ayer remarking that as soon as one had the answers, the subject was no longer philosophy. He also held that theorizing is a creative activity. It is to uncover elusive answers that you need imagination most. And was it Hume who came up with the delightful "To what question could this possibly be the answer?"?

Special questioning is triggered whenever a situation seems to be outside one's capability, never met before, or a 'wicked problem' as Michael Pacanowsky calls it. Then you need original thought. Thinking work is what the best people are supposed to be there for. My starting position is that I believe a useful leadership process should:

- Generate more possible solutions to a problem than someone would do otherwise
- Develop the solution until it actually works
- Make evaluation and choice of the best idea more confident
- Encourage the contribution of other people in finding the solution
- Increase the commitment of all who will need to implement it
- Let the person(s) involved feel in control of it.

Chapter 3
Your Strategic Approach

There is an ever-present competition between imagination, emotion and reason, in striving to find Truth. Yet mostly we want to think only as little as necessary, always feeling short of time. What do we see as of pressing relevance now? One needs to choose between three levels of a kind of 'Relevance Box'. Should I confine myself to reason, or take account of human feeling, or will I need to go beyond these to the realm of wonder? Where to begin, and in what order is best?

1. Three moral struggles

Truth is at the center of a triangle of competing forces. Severe tensions between imagination, reason and emotion present us with moral struggles over our integrity. More people value reason than imagination, but the dichotomy is false—it's a matter of information and timing—and imagination must be used with intelligence, else it is not really creative.

Figure 3.1. Moral struggles

Imagination

TRUTH

Reason   Emotion

Imagination is usually anathema to Reason, but they act like a door that must both open and close, like breathing in and out. One offers judgment, the other its opportunity to consider beyond what is already known to be true. It's a conflict between doubt and hope, but disciplined creativity wins the palm.

Imagination is never having to say it's impossible. Reason is conservative and safe, Imagination ambitious and willing to risk. When it comes to knowledge of the truth, Reason thinks it has enough to decide on, whilst Imagination aspires to find new clues to a solution.

Reason and Emotion, each essential to judging the best thing to do, face a great moral dilemma: which should be stronger, 'how good is this idea?' or 'how well will it work?'? Is it really 'moral' to choose what delivers high-minded values, in the knowledge it hasn't a chance; or is life, like politics, the art of the possible? "Do right, whatever comes of it." Shares in tobacco bring best returns, but…

To pit emotion against intelligence always fails, so it is just foolish—yet that is what most people do, leading to heated arguments. We face conflict between head and heart; what we need and what we want; the letter of the law versus the spirit; relationships forged from either respect or love. As with the concepts of 'socio-technical divide' and 'user-interface design,' it's no use bringing out a technically efficient product which users cannot handle or society will not embrace. The only solution is to find a way through by improving the information deployed, to explore more unusual approaches, or of course to transcend the whole thing.

Emotion may drive Imagination to find better solutions, and it is emotional energy that gets things done. But it will oppose any idea unless it feels good or has appeal to people. It is the engine of both desire and fear, and so might hold you back because your idea does not suit or live up to its values, beliefs, interpretations or predictions.

Emotion is the push from close inside yourself, whilst Imagination is the pull from outside, which has to be free from the duty to discover only what will turn out to appeal. It is crucial to go first for ideas before ensuring acceptability. The latter will usually become essential, although it prevents an invention or initiative becoming innovated. Anything not familiar invites suspicion, and trust is king. In practice Imagineers, consumed with pursuit of an exceptional result, do not pay enough attention to people issues, so their idea sometimes falls away.

The essential bridge between the opposing mindsets of reaching for the idea and winning agreement and support is therefore in how the information gets put across.

To sum up, what is true is not always right. Values can easily work against you so you have to choose between free will and wise will. "*People want what is good, but they don't always see it*" (Jean-Jacques Rousseau in Social Contract). Ideals that don't work cannot stand. This is why awareness of how you are thinking about the realities facing you is so crucial. No judgment should be allowed whilst reaching for a new idea, else you will stop yourself finding anything exceptional. But to judge is essential after you have found it—else you are in danger of acting on it!

2. How to think as little as necessary

Nearly forty years ago, I was headhunted by an international consultancy who could lay some claim to being exceptionally effective in the field of rational thinking. This was Kepner-Tregoe Inc. and I joined as Managing Director of their UK operations, which I then extended into Europe and Scandinavia. I already knew their work at first hand and it commanded my respect, and still does. However, when using their methodology a strange thing could be seen to take over, if people did not take care to bring in some countervailing energy. Too rigid a dedication to rationality seemed to deaden the soul, to harden the categories, even to alter the countenance. It was comparable to the effect computers can have if you become too addicted to them. Some of the human joy goes out of life, and some of the beauty.

The remorseless grinding of the logic-machine, the piercing force and accuracy of specific questioning, the sense of knowing that there was no flaw in the reasoning but the answer was still 'wrong' all caused me to question how much of reality could be governed by reason alone. At the same time, a pattern began to emerge in the reactions of the more senior people I worked with in client companies. "This logical and specific system of thinking is unarguable on its own terms, but..." They were recognizing there was more to thinking than sheer or mere reasoning, but they couldn't exactly systemize how they thought, label it or describe it well. These experiences spurred me to go in search of whatever it was that might be outside that tight cage. What was needed for fuller understanding of how to realize one's potential? I thought this would be imagination or creativity or innovation, but there was also something else...

Relevance and confidence combine to affect "how to think as little as possible and as much as necessary," surely an elegant objective. We are usually willing to increase our effort and go deeper into things only if we begin to lose confidence in succeeding without more work! It is curious that although attention span is a measure of low or high intelligence, a top executive too often denies himself what would bring quality and breadth/span/stretch, because s/he has no time. They live on the headlines, relying on those who prepare executive summaries to have done the front-line thinking. Time is money and Churchill wanted it all on half a page. "Get to the gist," or "I've already made up my mind." *Some barristers read their brief on the train as they travel to court.*

3. No time to think?
The first thing is to win time. Every day of your life, you find yourself facing a kaleidoscope of problems. They certainly don't come in orderly fashion, and if they don't come to you, you tend to create them by setting fresh goals or standards, or by imagining what might happen in the future. It is always wise to think before you act; always. The question is, what kind of thinking will raise our chances of success, and for how long that will be worthwhile. Act too quick: repent at leisure.

'How much time is it worth?' is down to

$$\frac{\text{Importance x difficulty}}{\text{Time}}$$

But our lives are so busy, under pressure, thinking is normally done on the run, skimming the surface. If it's familiar, we react on instinct or habit, with 'do it again' or 'more of the same.' This might work, and if so it frees our attention for other situations more difficult, new or important. Frequent practice produces skill, enabling people to do things apparently without effort; or we get it in a flash and know what connects with what, and so do what it takes. One can dictate a report while driving to the office, and I've ceased to be amazed by how busy people now have a cell phone clapped to their ear while crossing the street. Systems and procedures, like forms for oft-recurring activities, are (cleverly) designed to reduce having to think from scratch each time, yet assure effective results.

"All animals are equal, but some are more equal than others," declared the pigs in George Orwell's *Animal Farm*. Relevance says this of information, assuring that how you address a problem has a direct bearing on whatever information you use. It's no use obeying the old-fashioned manager who tells you to "first get all the facts." Adroit use of thinking enables you to identify stuff that is distinctive or special, which saves an awful lot of useless legwork and wasted time. Information may lie far outside what is apparently relevant yet some data may actually turn out to be crucial.

We think the more furiously, deeply, wide and fast, the more serious the situation facing us. '*When in doubt, out*' can also mean to think else before committing rash deeds. Sometimes our own values clash with one another so badly we are stuck—damned if we do this, damned if we do that, dead if we do nothing. As soon as we aren't sure what to do for the best, we'd better think first. And anyway, thought is the least risky, the most economical, the most ambitious gainer and at best the fastest thing we ever do: you can think to Mars and back faster than the speed of light.

4. Three levels of relevance

Some readers might wish to visit Chapter 14 on the Relevance Box. What else could it mean to go 'outside the box?' If you need to think as little as possible, go for the security of the Reduction Box. But causality is central to invention, discovering new ways to bring something about. This requires we put the Reduction Box into a (larger) Relevance Box, to stretch from the immediate and the probable to entire wonder.

For thinking to be efficient, recognize you can do it from three differing levels, A, B and C below. I have even named the types of people who characteristically like to spend more time and effort on each one of these three: Reasoners, Feelers and Imagineers.

Figure 3.2. Three levels of approach

C. Wonder: What Else?

To seek a new way

Dazzling Imagineers

B. The Stronger Box of Feel: Why?

To dis/like it

Warm Feelers

A. Reductionist Box of Reason: How?

To be sure

Cool Reasoners

A. The Reductionist Box of Reason

Reasoners rely on *how* things ought to work, so as to be sure; Feelers give weight to *why* things matter to people; Imagineers wonder if something *else* might be better. Most people have a strategic or archetypal preference between these three levels. But confidence comes before a fall, so we'd better bother with what people feel, and might even need to seek the unusual. But when?

Now, suppose you wish to be very sure of success. You would narrow your focus down to whatever action seemed most familiar, similar, and close by, and most immediate, likely and obvious. You'd squeeze your thinking into the box of Reductive Relevance. It is safer to hold to the facts you know and support with logic and reason, so that whatever you choose to do deserves to work, and you know How. People invest in thinking further only when immediate or obvious solutions don't seem sure enough.

B. The Stronger Box of Feel

Should we ignore the people concerned: WHY could they oppose or support the conclusion reached by reason alone? Our objective Relevance Box must surely extend into a Stronger one, to include their subjective and personal feelings. Ignore these at your peril, for the power of their emotions may easily overwhelm mere rationale, whether it be for or against you. This becomes a crucial factor for innovation, when the warm, subjective feelings of the people inside and the market outside can over-rule cool, objective reason.

Should the Reductive or the Stronger Box be in charge? *Professor Jones had a delightful tale to tell of the rocket-testing project carried out in Sweden and how risk was handled. Government decided to use the sparsely populated and remote north of the country, and to make doubly safe, they would bring away all the Sami by helicopter from Lapland down to Stockholm or Gothenburg, where accommodation would be provided for the duration of the rocket-launchings.* So far so good. But Jones quickly points out that the risk was thus multiplied on a massive scale. The chance of even a reindeer actually being hit in the vast north was extremely low; the risk of a helicopter crash was many times more; and the threat to the northern people of catching some disease would be quite high. Yet if they did not airlift them out, the slightest hitch would hit the headlines and condemn the callousness of Government. Human considerations of course won out: emotion can overcome reason.

The Cool Reductive Box ensures only that whatever we choose to do should work in the objective world outside: but often we must listen to the Warm half of the famous Man/Machine interface. After all, any faculty that carries sins like greed, lust, avarice, envy, pride, sloth and gluttony packs a lot of power! Nobody said that Stronger implies goodness: it's just that it can often overwhelm logic, and to hell with the logic of numbers.

C. Wondering beyond the Box

The most bloody battles in coming to a decision are fought between those Reasoners and Feelers. But the third level of our Relevance Model opens up into a wider world, the unusual universe beyond or outside the box of normality. Welcome Wonder. When reason and feeling cannot resolve the issue, the only recourse is to think else or otherwise. Some people feel the three levels as cold, warm and bright, from pure logic, through human feeling to spiritual freedom.

Behold! This ancient word, perhaps out of date today, crystallizes the spirit of surprise and awe we feel when something new and wonderful is before us.

The science fiction writer Sir Arthur C. Clarke declared that if a scientist tells you something is possible, he is probably right. If he says it is impossible, probably wrong.

When the obvious is not satisfying your need, what stops you from even the wildest speculation? You have nothing to lose. How could you possibly attempt to judge an idea before you have even reached it?

Naming these three 'characters' makes the people you deal with very easy to recognize. **Reasoners** want to be sure of what to do very early, reasoning with facts, 'wasting' no more time outside the objective physical world of How things ought to work. Yet this is so often why decisions fail or plans go wrong. **Feelers** believe in considering what people feel about the situation, Why it matters to them and why they would want to contribute. This question certainly secures a second dimension, and it is often worth more time to assure people's motivation.

Finally, come the ones who wonder, who seek the unusual. Eager to push further out for other possibilities, other objectives or criteria, less obvious risks, and so on, exploring wider, deeper and further for such ideas, all these could be named **Imagineers.** These go strong on what Else? Our database on *Rhodes' Thinking-Intentions Profile* shows the last as being in a minority, and because people so often act naturally from their default position, it is no surprise that imagination plays second-fiddle in most management work.

Of course everyone has to go there when in desperation, or when spurred by aspiration. But the beauty of wonder is that it acts as a third dimension to thought, achieving so much more gain for less cost. Its unusual questions and imagery bring many complex thoughts together, simply, and may even infuse the rest of your mental faculties… It also takes short cuts that can produce amazing results without deserving to!

II
Awareness through imagery

Chapter 4
The Birth of an Idea: Awareness

An idea either simply comes to you or you may strive for one, going from passive Receiver to pro-active Searcher. When being conceived it is little more than a nebula. You decide whether to ignore and reject it or to focus your attention, and if it seems worthwhile and immediate, allow some feeling to form, usually at least coloured by what's in your memory. One can recognise seven Stages of Awareness, though not always in sequence. How thoughts arise is actually complex, iterative and overlapping, and unlike this slow-motion account, often swift.

Making yourself aware is a mind-switch skill that offers control, and you drive it with your intention to learn. Some don't bother, but you can always change and enlarge your images of perception on purpose.

A. Stages of Awareness

   1. An observation or encounter is sensed or suffered:
    Aha! I experience some change—it is so

    2. An impression made by this experience:
     Yes, I notice it now—I feel it

     3. Conscious attention*:*
      Oh, I am aware this matters

      4. Recognition:
      I would know this again

       5. Personal insight:
       I feel what this means…for me

        6. A new hypothesis forms:
        Could it be that…?

         7. Commitment:
         Take it further

1. Observation: *Aha! I experience some surprise or change*

The stimulus for serious thought is to notice some contrast between what is happening or has happened and what might or should be. Is it a threat or an opportunity? Thinking is triggered by surprise, something we are not ready for, and if emotion is involved, there's a knee-jerk reaction. We don't properly know why, yet the emotion is often the most real thing there is. On the other hand, when an idea strikes us, we know it is not real, but just something that might become so. There is no need to believe in it, since it has just arrived in our mind, from goodness knows where, and is so new we cannot know enough about it yet.

Attention is aroused as soon as one feels the need to act on what is going on. Paying attention to one's 'work' is a hallmark of highly skillful people. What activates awareness is driven by what interests them, at the moment, and they focus energy on what they are sensing passively, because it resonates with something within them. Even when I ignore something, I am reducing my focus on it on purpose and so I am actually giving it attention—you need to decide <u>not to</u> look at the elephant in the room. But if it matters enough, one moves from unconscious passive Receiver to conscious pro-active Searcher mode, and then pretty fast to intention.

Much of our thought process comes directly from the way we experience the world physically, in space and time. Awareness, or mindfulness, is the mental version of seeing, hearing, feeling, and noticing the relationships between what we observe. Imaginative people tend to score higher than most on noticing and sensitivity to events, if not to people (but that's another story.)

2. Impression: *Yes, I notice it now—I feel it*
Even as some 'cloud of unknowing,' it makes enough impression to attract my attention and perhaps connect with stored memories. I may develop some inkling, using any of my senses, to make it more tangible. For instance, to catch the image I may paint a picture, grope for words, or find some other way to represent it: tunes are great for recalling a memory.

This is the raw image as observed—direct and immediate. Every moment of the day we are being bombarded from outside by such assaults on our senses, large and small. Whether not real or true, any first impression is real to me and may be extremely strong, vivid and lasting. I can also suffer the same impact from *inside* my mind when conceiving an idea or when changing or combining existing images. Although this sensing may take time to emerge, at some point I feel 'struck' by it, and this consciousness determines whether to attend to it or not. Engaging my feeling converts impression into idea.

Figure 4.1. An idea realized

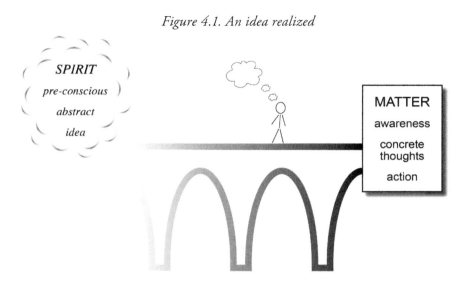

3. Conscious attention: *Oh, I am aware this matters and I doubt I can handle it.*

Attention is focused because it is relevant—does it matter or not? This may be spurred by a yawning gap between what is and what should be, caused either by some new ambition or by loss of confidence, the feeling of being uncertain whether things are going well enough. One day, Ernest Rutherford called together his team at Cavendish Laboratory to tell them there was no budget left – so there was nothing for it but to start thinking! Some last resort! Far from it: for a century, the Cavendish has been famous for the firsts in science it has produced, traditionally with few physical resources. Could they still do it without even a shoestring?

Doubt is coupled with dis<u>satis</u>faction, and *satis* means 'enough.' Needless to say, it is the nature of thought-leaders to keep setting ambitious new directions, creating their own dissatisfaction. Thinking entails a construction <u>inside</u> the mind to suit the situation faced in the world <u>outside</u>. These are two systems that collide when we feel disappointment and we empathize with when all feels OK. We seek a good (enough) matching between them, a conclusion that will work, an action that succeeds in dispelling the turbulence so that we have achieved a kind of inner peace or 'happiness'—at least for the time being.

Figure 4.2. Inner and outer worlds

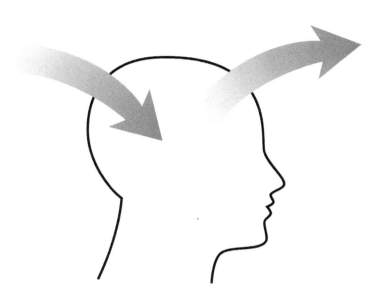

So we must ever align our internal and external worlds, producing harmony between our <u>being</u> and <u>becoming</u> inside the mind and our <u>doing</u> in the world outside: it goes both ways.

4. Recognition: *I would know this again*

How do we find a file or email, without some name, image or container making it repeatable? Recognition requires some way to categorize things as similar or different. It is possible to have read or heard a word or witnessed an event, but be unable to re-cognize it (know it again). This simply means that the image of an experience you had encoded didn't work. That's why it's good to capture feelings, concepts or notions out of thin air, to do something with them and give them physical form. Images, as a form of 'language,' process and convey our thoughts. Even yellow sticky notes help.

5. Insight: *I feel what this means…for me*

When I realize something for the first time, 'it dawns on me.' We sense impressions, feel values and emotions, intuit possibilities without evidence. All these 'soft' intimations might be called 'a feeling of.' We notice the flavor of a scene or situation or a message; the feeling of practical grasp at a do-able level—"this is about as much leverage as I am strong enough to handle."

> *"Know what you only almost-know, before or*
> *instead of realizing its meaning and reality."*
> J M W TURNER, ENGLISH PAINTER

6. Imagined hypothesis: *Could it be that…?*

Until this point, the 'common currency' running through these levels of awareness has been imaging. Consciousness has been growing as I pull together all the images received so far into proper thought. Imagination then allows making connections with other images normally far apart, to produce some new idea. Homeopathy seems to go against the stream of logic when asserting that extremely small doses can be made more effective than large ones. This needs me to sever links with those (medical) theories I already have, open up to anything, and just pretend something might be true. Making new connections feels not unlike magnetism or electrical energy with some sense of fusion, perhaps almost a sexual consummation. No wonder a new hypothesis is pictured as a light-bulb.

7. Ownership of a thought: *It should be done*

Any idea can be ignored, put to one side to consider later, modified or simply rejected. You cannot possibly know whether it's any good until you have reached it. Anyone promising to conceive only good ideas would hardly ever reach one. As Einstein trenchantly observed, "If we knew what we were doing, it wouldn't be called *research*." Commitment to it in advance would be a real gamble, with the odds against at many to one.

Further still, everyone has had that instant feeling of conceiving a winner, only to realize soon after that it's actually a loser. Wicked notions have tempted even great saints—but one can be blamed for them only if those temptations are entertained!

Any idea needs competition with others, to reveal how good or bad it might be, so you should never stop after the first one. Taking ownership means to abandon existing constructs and alternative ideas, so as to commit to something new and (hopefully) 'better.' Whenever we Realize or become conscious of something, the 'ize' means to <u>make</u> real in the mind, just as to energize means to <u>make</u> or produce energy.

Imagination, as leader of thought, must now be acted upon, so we become more aware. We "stiffen the sinews, summon up the blood," alert, on top form, crystallizing a sense of direction and commitment. Now my feelings belong to me, for I am exerting my will, energy and ability, and so do my ideas. I commit to do my best, see it through, steer my efforts back on course to success. In short, I am 'up for it.' *Effectiveness can be likened to the bending of a cross-bow; intelligence to the quality of your aim; and decisiveness to the releasing of the trigger* (after Sun Tzu, *The Art of War*).

Why imagination is such a huge matter is that it comes from and engages the whole mind, not simply the brain. There is something more than cognitive about it. Being awake and aware comes from fear, assuring our very survival. But imagination will also focus attention, make use of memory, enable you to exercise free will, the hallmark of humanity. Mankind has evolved to be greater than plants and trees, insects and animals, to have aspirations, make long distance plans, be driven by its own intentions and decide what these should be.

B. From passive receiving to active striving
1. Active or passive?
When you receive an idea without trying, count yourself lucky. For sure, awareness of how one is thinking helps you to go on the offensive, even to manipulate your own mind and all its senses, on purpose and at will, so that it all comes together beautifully in something new and practical.

> "The violin bow tells you what to do" (violinist).
> "If it's a good bow, it will teach you how to play" (violin maker)

Passive thoughts are ones we suffer or allow, so we receive some thoughts willy-nilly: they may blurt out on us or steal in from outside; as they are unbidden, we can neither claim credit for nor be responsible for their entering our mind. We may be victims of habit, conventions, rules, and unconscious assumptions. When an idea just pops into the mind, it will behave more like an instinct or an emotion than a thought, until we decide to entertain it and take it on. You can follow your impressions or lead with your thought. In passive mode, we respond to implied suggestion, in active mode to explicit command.

How do you get an idea to happen to you? Maybe you can invite and attract it, make yourself welcoming, alert to listening whenever the idea might fall on you. 'Early adopters' are usually hopeful, quick to see the potential in something. Spinoza distinguished events that happen to us or around us from those we cause on purpose—politicians nowadays so often attempt to escape blame for their wrong actions by saying their (unfortunate) deeds or results just 'happened'! Certainly you can sense things and try to make sense of things; you can see or look, hear or listen, feel the wind or feel for it by wetting your finger. As Polanyi would say, some ideas you hear or receive tacitly, or use without thinking about what you are doing; others you can put to good use on purpose and with your eyes open. Rather than be some hapless victim of experiences, you can take control.

You can notice an impression but ignore it, you can take it up, or you can reject it. You can treat an insight as threat or opportunity, as clearing fog, or simply with curiosity. It may turn into the excitement of potential and being valued as useful, though this is unlikely unless it really matters. Generally, our feelings and desires push, whilst reason pulls us, and to achieve resonance between them is masterly! The fairground machines that give everyone such an exciting ride make some people terrified, so that they accompany their children only by mustering all their resolve to give them a good time. Even swings can be daunting. Yet I found that by taking over the movement of the swing or the roller coaster, and willing even more impetus rather than holding back on it, I could just about manage to survive my fear.

Being creative means to get ideas to 'happen to me' on demand, being in the driver's seat where I can steer what I do to align it with my will. Equally, I can remain in charge even when assaulted. "To be angry is to be wrong" (Hugh Kingsmill). When you are angry, realizing it can alter your state of mind and therefore what you actually do about it. So the wise person can say calmly "I am feeling furious about you now" and thereby make it possible to deal with the situation better. Consciousness lends self-control, even in real-time pressure. Indeed, when in denial we may repress or disown an undesirable reality to escape being dominated by it, instead of summoning the strength to dominate it.

2. Turning perception into active output

To take the purposeful initiative, to actively reach for a brilliant idea, we need a different approach that alters the balance of intention from being pulled to pushing, or from following your impressions to leading with your thought. Since hidden assumptions can so bias, steer and limit our experiencing, why not make the most of new awareness of them, for a new purpose? Let's put impressions to work by creating wrong ones and turn this to advantage, for there's a huge potential or opportunity. When facing a problem, Robinson Crusoe looked around his island, asking *What would be good for that?* But also he went through the tools he had rescued from the shipwreck, to ask *What would this be good for?* Turning away from what is familiar directs the eye towards possibilities for the strange. Suddenly I see different relatedness or a surprising causal connection, and experience the excitement of uniting the emerging idea with what I need. Got it!

Being aware of the images lurking in your head is critical for getting new ones. Impressions are only an involuntary 'Input' so it's worth exploring how to make <u>active</u> perceptions, seeking 'Outputs' that are new, unusual or different. *Black swans really do exist, so why not a scarlet snowdrop?* Perception can be a transformer device. <u>What</u> you see depends heavily on <u>how</u> you look at it, so exploit this gestalt. "The dark night of the soul is a source of light: out of what you have or are comes what you have not and might become" (Mother Teresa). Truth lies somewhere in between the person, the object, and its comparator. A film about the Battle of Stalingrad made by a Russian is bound to differ hugely from one written by a German. This 'inside-out' approach can open the way to treating apparent 'fact' with the infinite flexibility required for originality. Anything that is not really 'there' might require to be imagined.

Sometimes, one becomes the lucky receiver of an original notion—a gift. So listen out for when the idea might fall on you. Or simply approach an old idea anew.

3. Learning

How many times do we fail to 'learn the lesson' of our own experience, never mind that of others? Learning itself entails a widening of awareness. "The cultivation of imagination should be the chief aim of education—just where it is failing" (Mary Warnock). Imagination is the fundamental means for learning what we don't know or believe. Just as Hooke's microscope and Galileo's telescope opened up the enlargement of scale, we do now have some instruments, language and tools to explore discovery further.

Learning works in a virtuous circle. They say one learns through doing, but one can learn bad things to do, and learn to do things badly! What happens is that one notices the effects of activity (what Kolb called reflective observation) and then one should interpret what caused them (abstract conceptualizing). Once you realize that this enables you to do it again better, you have begun to learn, perhaps with active experimentation, or trying things out. What separates the sheep from the goats is that the sheep apply any new concept to a range of apparently 'different' cases elsewhere, because they can conceive a less obvious similarity. Sadly, most people are goats, without such imagination.

Change the world? Then begin with yourself! for you are the only one who can change your values. *If the mountain will not come to Mahomet…* Maybe faced with global warming, even developed nations will discover that 'small is beautiful.' Converting the bad into the good needs simply a switch of attitude or outlook, perhaps being subversive in a good cause. When you feel cold and too poor to turn on the heating, put on extra clothing instead. *We change the behavior of a neutrino by looking at it.* This relativity applies not only to our sensing in the physical world but also to making sense within our minds.

In the Stronger Box in Chapter 3, we discussed how our personal feelings and perceptions determined Relevance. So one can feed imagination by purposefully widening perception, and becoming more creative about our values and goals, rather than focusing on material ways to satisfy them. It is not unknown for people to actually have their house moved to somewhere they now prefer to live. Now we can have our office in the palm of our hand, or work from wherever we want to live, just as it has become smart to run a small car or re-cycle our water. How many flights could a company cut out by achieving the real objective of each journey in some other way? The relentless rise of aspiration makes it more and more vital to attain a harmonious resonance between what we feel we need and what has to be done to get it.

"You <u>can</u> use business for good" I recently heard said earnestly on radio. What on earth was the image she had in her head about the reasons for founding and carrying on a business? Maybe, when the original business grows big, it loses sight of its original purpose to give something to the world…

When creative, you extend your experience beyond its normal reach. You distort what you know or sense, in time, shape, direction or force. You make gaps that weren't there and bridge others with great mental leaps. One can also decide the purpose of the image one is making: to be true to reality, to reflect a certain value, or to project a future fantasy. A map of the world as it might be in AD 2100 will differ from a real geographic map, and also from one infused with politics. Think of the notorious one by Fred Rose showing Europe in the tentacles of a giant octopus—the 'evil empire' of Russia. Even the European Union may be seen as the evil empire! A hallmark of the use of intelligence is the continual finding of patterns in whatever we come across. The child looking out of the window from her bed sees the branches of the tree outside. Especially when the leaves are gone in winter, she finds all sorts of interesting shapes—a lion, a boat, grandfather—and can even see some of the same shapes next day. Who is to say they are not there?

Chapter 5

Heighten your Sensing

People think, not just with their head and heart but also with their legs and arms, whose memory builds skill. The cross-references we make between our senses, and the workings of emotion, multiply the variety of images we can develop, and like analogy create a short-cut to learning.

Creative people are usually seen as 'sensitive', perhaps because they enrich their experiences more than most. It's good to heighten your senses in every way, not only through aesthetics and the arts, and develop 'tools' that magnify your skill each time you use them. Always be alert to an idea that seems to come not from thinking but only felt, as if from the spirit rather than the brain. Milk it for all you're worth.

Very clever people can be tempted to rely too much upon their heads, not enough on their legs. But it's a great mistake to cut our self off from physical sensitivity, for that sensitivity encourages ideas we would not normally have! The civilized sophistication of the townsman can treat physical senses as obsolete, and leave behind the country ways of his simple brother, unaware that the latter draws upon a wide range of subtle skills. Creative people are often more aware than others, and connect to ideas both by analogy and by literal feeling. Prepositions such as with, from, to, under, above, beside are about physical, spatial reality, yet they show grammar as a model for much of thought itself. Whilst Jung could separate thinking from feeling and sensing from intuition (and Myers Briggs followed him), a practical focus on imagination shows you should feed them all into one another. If you want ideas, access more experience from the less visited parts of your memory and intensify your sensing faculties, using them as amplifiers of that experience.

1. Exploit our memory resources

First, transform what you have: imagination lies inside you, not outside. All physical matter is finite and indestructible, and what scientists do is to transform it from one shape or structure to another. So why not transform our 'memory' simply by making different connections or pathways between various items in it? A would-be creative person without a rich storehouse of experience is as lost as an inventor without metal or chemicals. This storehouse is where ideas come from. You do not stand in the middle of some metaphoric ocean or desert, looking desperately for ideas. It is more like searching for a gift in the vast warehouse of junk and antiques within your memory. Let's pursue this analogy here, supposing you want to buy a present for a friend.

Purpose: *you must know why you are giving this present, who it's for and what is the occasion.*
Criteria: *you might not know exactly why the right present will please her, but you should certainly try to know how you'll recognize a good one when you see it.*
Assumptions and habits: *your warehouse probably has well-worn corridors that would lead you to thinking of gifts often purchased, such as perfume, chocolates, roses, tickets to a show.*
Try a new association, *with mind-set open to any options: if you haven't got much money, you might go for an unusual present, which brings its own merits. You could seek some category that will produce a 'find,' and thus provide a surprising*

extra joy for your friend. An invitation to join the space program, or perhaps an orchestra??

Of course, the richer your warehouse of experience, the more chances to sort them all into new combinations. This is why some parents make great efforts to give their children the widest range of experience they can afford.

In this analogy, perceiving this find is the essence of having a creative idea. So, to exploit imagination, use better labeling, more cross-references, and actively keep your eyes open wider when searching your inner files.

Another booster is to foster the 'snowball effect,' where experience is likened to snow. From birth, everyone accumulates in their head everything they encounter. This snowballs, as the more someone knows the more there is for new experiences to stick to. But those who put out extra feelers, like twigs stuck into their snowball, will accumulate extra snow, or experience, as they roll. So find any tools and questions to trigger new ideas and variations, so as to extend your perceptions. Begin to collect and make your own favorites. Recognize what is often shared by exceptionally inventive solutions, and glean the lessons from them. Twigs like those grow your snowball even more exponentially. The following chapters will try to explore various ways to do this.

2. Latent power of our physical resources

Heightened alertness and sensitivity to impression fuels imaginative notions. Those who wish to see had better look; to hear had better listen; to feel had better touch; to smell had better sniff, and to taste had better savor around the mouth. The whole person has a body as well as a head, hands as well as spirit. Aristotle actually advised the separation of brainwork from physical exercise, but *have you ever considered what it took to come up with the design of an anvil—or even a shovel?* What a blacksmith cannot fashion with that strange shape is hardly worth listing, so he has conceptual skills of a high order.

Actually the 'lower order' sensory attributes give a person astonishing mental short cuts. We still only dimly realize that we learn by doing and watching the results, not just by thinking. Some surgeons would not like to see themselves as craftsmen or barbers, and educationists expect too much learning through abstract concepts alone. The whole education system in Britain is still assuming that the intellectual skills that (should) develop from an academic discipline are generic enough to suffice for everyone and every kind of work, job, calling and career. Nonsense. Many of the social needs of the service industry, and jobs demanding physical tools to be allied with practical thinking, require education that is not only different but also goes wider. Even in Parliament, it is *all talk and no show,* so that debates are less effective and go on for hours too long. If only they would try making their thoughts and speeches more visible and tangible, for the brain has severe limits on the complexity it can handle on its own.

Physical stimulus to release inner potential is needed for both emotional and practical reasons. Taking motivation first, we need the spur of immediacy. Physical experience seems closer and more real than an abstract idea, because it is alive. Heinz Wolff, Professor of Bioengineering at Brunel, speaking of invention on BBC, advocated, "Have clever hands—but in your brain."

I too see the mind as a lot more than the brain, which it embraces, along with the body, and their continuous interactions. Craftsmen, sportsmen and all skillful people actually learn to think through the need for managing and coordinating multi-physical movements. I once twisted my leg muscles just by pulling on the starter cord of a lawnmower; when you jump a five-bar gate, how many of your limbs and muscles are working in harmony with your leg? Caroline Tosh, a top cranial osteopath told me, "I'm listening to your knee."

It is our senses that naturally bridge emotion and imagination. Language transfers across our five senses, for instance, when we 'feel' something, it might be through our emotions, or through our fingers, kinetically. A literal image is what we see with our eyes, an emotion what we feel or hear with our hearts, an idea that does not (yet) exist but is just conceived in the mind's eye. We sense things with our fingertips, when 'hearing' the music behind the words, when scenting victory in a World Cup rugger match, even when we feel the sweet taste of revenge. We can have a feeling that something might exist or might happen, when it is neither an emotion nor what we can feel with our hands. Even the word 'intuition' is used to denote an uncanny prediction, a kind of knowing without any concrete evidence, or the famous 'woman's intuition,' which might actually arise from extremely close observation of subtle signals emitted by another person. Sensing may indeed be the means to invite images into our consciousness and to welcome and notice them when they come. Through imagination, we can go anywhere without being there—and from there we can see where we are. "Steeple Bumpstead may not be the end of the world, but you can certainly see it from there!" Of course, jokes don't always work...

3. Physical sensitivity and its variety

If, in social settings, 80% of mental energy is stimulated aurally, does 80% of intellectual direction originate visually? *Nobody would think of painting even a base board without a good light, else you cannot see how you are doing, what patches you are leaving thin and where you are going over the line, without 'cutting in' skillfully with the fine line of your brush.* Sight is the most obvious of all the senses to be working 'at a distance'—you can look all the way up a street for a chemist, or see something a million miles away without going there; so we taste failure, hear the words between the lines, feel the scope, see the vision, don't like the sound of this or the flavor of that, and so on. In fact, to think with, we resort to tangible senses. Hearing offers less scope to objectify something, to change its shape and other characteristics, because sound doesn't last—unless recorded by musical notation or through electronics. Even memories are in need of physical capture, quantification and storage, as in words, numbers or pictures, including metaphors. Smell is not the only sense that determines taste. Curiously, how something tastes may be influenced by the size or thickness of, for instance, chocolate, or the shape, as in pasta, where a cylinder tastes different from the exact same mixture made flat; good tea simply should not be offered in thick crockery, nor wine in plastic mugs!

Figure 5.1. A cat's whiskers

Jonathan Spence said that Zhanng Dai, the historian (1597–1680) was a connoisseur of tea so refined that he could tell which river the water had come from. Human water tasters are still more accurate than their instruments. I also remember that in the 1960s the precision and control of lens polishing machinery in Rank Precision Industries had reached its limits, so the ultimate finishing of a giant astro telescope lens was carried out by hand: we knew then of only 16 people in England who could do this refining task—better than a machine.

The word 'emotion' comes from the Latin *movere* to move, which we also use for being moved by heroism or grief. When we 'Observe,' all our senses are primitive receivers and senders of emotion. *When we think to speak, the voice-muscles in our throat can be seen working.* In sensing an impression, emotion or idea, the mind tingles in anticipation. Emotional shock can travel through the body to the most embarrassing extremity! This is without spiritual empathy and the magic of symbolism, metaphor, analogy, simile, etc. Dalton "used imagination as his microscope" and Robert Frost (in Poets on Poetry) said, "A sentence is a sound in itself on which other sounds called words may be strung." This led Tom Paulin to realize that, especially for a play, whatever he wrote should be speakable out loud so as to be fully comprehended. *A jellyfish possesses a sense-body with both visual and auditory functions* and our sense of touch adds quality to what we can appreciate with the eye. Yet some galleries and museums still prohibit the handling, stroking and fondling of sculptures such as Henry Moore's—which were <u>made</u> to be felt. (Let the acid effects from hands go hang, I say—or lose function in the sculpture itself.)

Beethoven, who was deaf since age 30, was able to continue writing music through his 'aural imagination' until he died in 1827 at about 57. Elgar's so-called 'sketches' of music were left after his death and taken up by another musician, Anthony Paine, who 'finished' his symphony. The redness of a dress has more than its dye—it is probably sexy—though we must remember that black is funereal in Europe but not in China, where white is actually used. The poem, as distinct from prose, relies mainly on tacit meaning, rather like our intuitive feel. Good art, and aesthetics in general, is more likely to be subtle than 'in your face.'

The metaphorical screen we deploy is far more than the best flat screen of any computer, however many pixels this might offer: it is not only three-or-more dimensional but also operates through all of our known senses plus a few others we have that are not yet well explored and defined. Your own senses come together to 'get' the relations between things. So thought aligns and connects the snooker table pocket and the hand, the ball and the cue, one's own ball and the positions of all the others; it assesses what happens if my shot succeeds, what if it fails so that I hand over the opportunity to my opponent? The beauty of these inner images and devices is that, unlike physical materials, the cost of changing and exploiting them is merely virtual—virtually nothing.

Images are ideal for recognizing and capturing some elusive idea or concept. Because they have not been defined or specified sharply, they can powerfully influence the unconscious mind, reaching parts of memory normally less accessible and thus acting as a fertile source of new ideas.

4. Senses and synesthesia

Gerald Edelman in Consciousness quotes John Locke: "A studious blind man…bragged one day, that he now understood what scarlet signified. Upon which his friend demanding what scarlet was? the blind man answered, 'It was like the sound of a trumpet'." What is passing through such synesthetic examples is something more spiritual than material, and we convey the commonalities by images.

In fact, today we are everywhere crossing the frontiers of the five senses, enabling us to show sound visually as voiceprints that are as accurate discriminators as fingerprints. In the same way, heat can be photographed and mapped, and, by applying different sets of 'rules,' infrared enables us to see in the dark and detect forgeries by 'seeing' the difference in the inks. But we could carry this synesthesia across further into our mental imaging, which may be how metaphor came about. *This proposal stinks; we have tasted victory and we want more; I hear what you are saying in this letter; we were touched by your generosity; Oh, I see.* When we are feeling down, we may receive 'strokes' from a sympathetic colleague, not so different from stroking your dog. More recently than Bishop Berkeley: *"If a Man speaks in the forest and there's no Woman there to hear him, is he still wrong?"* (Jack Bowen, …*The Philosophy of Bumper Stickers*). All imagery. I hope the point is made.

Though we might use words such as 'insight,' imagination is actually dealing also with 'impressions' (touch); tones (aural); 'flavor' (taste); and even the smell of a situation—all are a kind of metaphorical synesthesia. Taking just the three senses of sight, feel and sound, we find the same words often run across all three 'media.' We speak of bright light, a bright edge to an axe and bright sound; wool is soft but there is a soft line in a design and sound may be soft too; there is a rough sketch, rough blanket and rough voice; heavy shoulders, heavy weight and heavy breathing over the telephone; we talk of blue jazz or feeling blue as well as blue mountains in the distance. Such comparisons are everywhere, so that it's possible to see them as a form of metaphor. We can also readily refer to poetry in motion, the building of alliances, and so on. The ocean depths can be 'mapped' not only visually, but also in sound, heat and pressure so whales and fish can navigate without light. I remember as an athlete with my left leg in plaster, being advised to think about the left leg to strengthen it, while actually exercising the right. Now, a wheelchair steered just by the thoughts of the 'driver' has been invented.

5. The symbiosis of mind and body

In thinking about the word 'psychosomatic' *just consider (calmly) the role of the mind during sex between husband and wife.* If ever proof were needed! And recall how natural it is to know what the other is thinking… Some people are actually able to discern the aura surrounding a person, reflecting her mood and temperament. It might be that you sense the aura first, out of thin air, without enough information or reasoning to justify its appearance. Its outline is dim, vague and without substance, yet you feel excited about some nebulous idea coming upon you.

Your brain has vast reserves, most of which remain untapped, just like the muscles even of a highly developed athlete or sportsman—which is why training is undertaken, even by the naturally gifted. I can say from personal experience that an attack of polio may sever all connection between a muscle and the brain, and these neural/electrical contacts are never to be renewed (at the present state of medical science). Yet by drawing on all the muscle fibers hitherto unused, you can actually regain use of that limb. You can do the same with the under-used muscle-fibers of your brain! No person lives long enough to re-use the tiniest fraction of their experience in all the combinations critical for their own problems: we have to be selective. Lazy people lose out by selecting the same bits of their experience over and over again, but many 'new' ideas come from seeing events from a different angle, on a strange plane or dimension, joined up with things hitherto or normally viewed as alien or irrelevant. Man invented writing and the storing of the world's experience, yet so often neglects the skills of access to his own mind. Even professors may use their knowledge poorly, through an embarrassment of riches perhaps; while the simple man with only one tool may use what he has with such artistry as to compensate for what he has not. *G K Chesterton's story in* The Coloured Lands *featured the Spaniard stranded on a desert island, who had only his scythe—but he could do all manner of things with this, from shaving to killing wild goats or fishes. His modern companion with the pistol could do little, even while his few rounds of ammunition lasted.*

Our hard-wired genetic inheritance of autonomic and instinctual reactions, to help survival when there's no time for thought, have progressed from the ancient reptilian brain through our limbic system to the cerebral cortex. As we grow, we establish a network of thinking and actions that work and these are enriched by sensory experience, which not only brings us our knowledge, but also shows how to <u>use</u> it.

6. The whole mind
This electro-chemical system unites to remember pathways in the nervous system that have been traveled before, and these become organic pigeonholes

for data of all kinds. Some physical experience of 'doing it' is essential for learning, just as practice is essential for our limbs and muscles to 'learn' how to play the violin or sail over a pole-vault bar three times our own height. That physical feeling or experience itself brings a kind of image, the counterpart to the virtual experience offered by a picture that is only mental.

"You can't tell me that anyone ever actually writes a song. What you do is to light a candle and the angels bring it in" (songwriter on BBC, 21 May 2009). An engaging thought, but when you look out onto your lawn, you see how green it is, and half-imagine its smoothness, how cool it is in the hot sun, the perfume arising from its clover, perhaps even how sweet the taste. A cow would guess how succulent and sweet the taste, yet never imagine anything not there; and it's unlikely she will see a brown patch on it in her imagination, whereas you can visualize it in multi-colored stripes or any sort of variegated pattern, *and artists might even paint it in purple.* I think that someone blind from birth could never do that, unless somehow by analogy.

Creative people are usually seen as 'sensitive.' Although it's a travesty to suggest that creativity is to be found only in 'the arts,' all domains of art do major on more vivid impressions: they are readily alert to something in the streaming of experience. I remember an artist telling me "I feel a picture coming on": indeed whenever a revelation comes upon anyone, they feel their senses sharpen.

However, sensitivity may have three faces, interpersonal defensiveness, physical power and intellectual subtlety. First, defensive self-consciousness is a grievous handicap, so as soon as confidence and motivation waver, ideas die at birth. No pressure, then! When highly able people fall victim to this, in America it's called to 'choke.' Confident communication is important even on your own—think of writer's block!—but more so when working with others on a project. Like over-confidence and complacency, brutal insensitivity is no good either. But we can learn skills for separating criticism of an idea from the person uttering it, including what to do when on the receiving end! There are special ground rules on sensitivity when working together to reach original solutions.

Physical power might not be associated with sensitivity, though in many fields, such as sport or craftsmanship, excellence demands delicacy, which, strangely, requires power. Energy, motivation and our driving instincts are essentially physical in nature. This is not to suggest that the brutish hulk should be in charge of one's tiny mind, but the ability to draw deeply on elemental resources of the body is a great resource, whilst meditation and other disciplines can help more of your natural creative energy to flow out.

Thirdly, intellectual weapons such as analytical power, vital for creative thinking, can nonetheless wound others below the waterline, yet the sensitivity required for intellectual subtlety proves often to be the secret to a breakthrough: sometimes, it is the only-just different, rather than the dramatic, which can be significant. Sensitivity makes the most of paradox, of analogy, of thinking liquidly rather than in concrete chunks, just as fluidic pressure has advantages over mechanical cams and cogs.

7. Heighten your senses

There is enormous latent power lying within every person, and we should draw upon all faculties, including bodily ones, although these are not often found in eggheads! Whilst the eye restricts its field by focus, the ear has simultaneous and constant 3D access, 360 degrees, in all directions.

Sensory experience is working not only in the electrical 'little gray cells' of Hercule Poirot, but also in every limb and fiber and chemistry of the physical body. When someone goes blind, his senses of touch and hearing are called upon with especial intensity. This concentration is a key skill for imagination. *When you stalk a tiger, you hear the very pressure on a leaf; he might be stalking you!* It is possible to turn on your own power, as one can put on a mood almost like a physical cloak: you can actually bring on anger or grief by making certain physical moves, and just by concentration we can call up the inner equivalents of a magnifying glass or an amplifier. When a wine taster focuses fully, they can identify not only the grape but the vintner, the location and even whether the ground slope faces the morning sun to the east. High quality listening entails not just hi-fi equipment, optics or electronics, but a heightened form of attention. Try becoming super-sensitive for the moment; enroll more of your five senses and raise the quality of your perceptions. It does need practice, but you can also withdraw energy from less-needed parts of the body at will, and release higher energy on command. These are skills of the athlete, but of course they apply to the mind as well as the body. The mind is more flexible than any machine, and hence many times faster than it seems when you try to measure its speed—say at merely 125 instructions per second!

Much of the progress made by Man is down to the development and use of tools, which improve on what it's possible to do, observe and measure. Enhancing the sensitivity and scope of our inner tools helps exploit imagination.

What information we receive depends on our sensitivity at that moment: how many sensors are alert and in use, how much power is switched on, how close we feel to the event, or how distant. What is seen as 'simple' from one point might be complex from another level, as when a tree can be drawn in a few strokes, yet may have many thousands of leaves. Equally, the title of any book is representing all the complexity within its few hundred pages in an extreme form of simplicity. Similarly with many line drawings, such as Gary Hume's *Princess* (1996), so economical with line that there is none at all for one side of the face and only nostrils for the nose—yet we at once see in full the kind of person she is.

8. Go and Do it! A few practical tips
It is a needless restriction to use only your head for thinking. To find brilliant or ingenious solutions to problems, you need all-out energy, and all the sensing and spiritual qualities you can muster, as well.

Another trick is to turn to doing something (else) physical. When you're stuck or inspiration dries up, some form of practical activity can release the flow again. Only those who prefer to sit like gods on Olympus despise practical devices for stimulating ideas: the rest of us are glad of anything which helps us achieve, so we make sure to recognize a connection, capture the idea and nail it down to develop it later. Here are a few activities that might work for you. Some of them seem quite child-like—but they work for grown-ups too!

Get up from your chair and walk about or go somewhere else—changing your literal viewing-point can actually offer a new mental vision. Go and do something you really enjoy or throw yourself into hard labor or exertion, especially if rhythmic. Gladstone used to axe trees! Make concrete physical examples or models of what is otherwise hidden inside your head and hard to express. Using small cards to write on and then to move around assists flexibility more than the good old flipchart—and the effect can also be simulated on-screen. For some, just playing music does the trick.

Pictures and diagrams, to 'draw it in the sand' (or on your smart phone) give amorphous or ephemeral notions some shape and impact, so they last. Artists are famous for their sketches, studies and cartoons, which act rather as experiments; a favorite for me is the back of an envelope. Others may resort to another medium or approach, or another discipline altogether, with its different assumptions and rules.

Ideas often come during vacations, getting back to nature, the elements, open sea, mountains, or sleeping on it (incubation!). I confess to getting ideas when in church, or at a serious or boring concert! Others have them in the bath or with sex.

My father, when a painting was going well, would press on with it for hours 'while the iron was hot,' eating bananas to sustain him. Managers often put on the pressure by setting intermediate targets, goals, milestones and limits of time or resources, relying on the principle of extrusion. When on your own, keep switching between distraction and pressure, by doing something else altogether unrelated, and then focusing hard on the issue. Authors seek a publisher before writing the book, since their deadline makes sure they don't mess about forever making it better. What I find amazing is how often we get ideas in an inconvenient place, and that many inventions come in the most grotty workshops, rather than in beautifully streamlined and perfect laboratories.

It's as if the god of creativeness plots to make you flexible so that you escape the silos, or bend the restricting rules. The erasing rubber is a great tool to avoid inhibitions, and using waste paper or something already thrown away is as good as starting with a pencil rather than a pen. There is another option, perhaps even better: be willing to make countless versions, and keep them all in chronological order, not throwing any away. Some inventors even prefer doing untidy stuff to using Computer-Aided Design, especially at early stages. Top scientists backed by the power of CERN still revert to a blackboard and chalk sometimes! When you go in for 'brainstorming,' it is only practical to do this 'mind-wrestling' in short bursts, for your judgment is being totally suspended during these streams of association. The final stage of each flow of wild thinking is to capture just the ideas that look promising, so as to spend time on developing these into something that might work and win acceptance. A creative spark, or the germ of an idea in its vague cloud, is no good without the sharpness of reality. But all you need to go from invention to innovation is just one workable idea that might never have been found by conventional plodding reason.

Above all, just get started, from wherever, even some random place. Don't rely on being able to justify the order of march—in fact when writing a list, postpone numbering the points or thoughts, at first—a fatal mistake of 'well-trained' organizers. The Imagineer can do no wrong because he is not relying on being right. If you expect to get it right first time, expect then to have to do it again and again and again. And if you generate 57 varieties, re-group them into bunches of 7 ± 2! You need many ideas, but nobody can handle a long list!

9. Mental sensing and 'felt-thought'

When we sense a situation, we cannot always attribute the data being received to any one of our five senses. Yet it is real enough. Like intuition, or 'knowledge-without-reason,' we ignore it at our peril. We sometimes over-rule such things on the grounds that Man has made more progress than animals by doing so, for she has majored on reasoning, using mental symbolism as a spiritual substitute for one's 'animal' senses. This is to miss the trick. Even trees and shrubs sense the deadness of a branch nearby and will not grow towards it; whilst flowers near the house sense the sunlight and disappointingly turn their faces away from your window. Why should we take no notice of thoughts just because they are merely felt? They come in many varieties, including instincts, and only the fool discounts their 'subjectiveness.' The inexperienced person who dismisses anecdotal evidence, trying to be 'scientific,' needs to dig deeper and follow through better: just because it has not been published doesn't mean it is not true. And "Beware what you read in the paper!"

Whatever gets recorded in your brain can be amplified by using a more sensitive inner 'microphone' which will 'listen' harder and pick up impressions otherwise lost or blurred. You can decide to listen out with more attention for particular kinds of input, so as to catch the original signal, and then to add further definition or descriptive analysis by the quality of energy you apply in processing it. With your real music system, sensitive equipment such as the microphone, amplifier, the tape, speakers and even the box itself will add sharper definition and quality of tone. Equally you can tune up your mind to act as a high fidelity system.

Physical sensitivity is a function of the number of sensors, their density and their inter-connections. We have many more sensors in our fingertips, lips and erogenous zones than on our back, and the interactions between brain and body are legion. To scientifically design a space for nil sound reflection is highly complex. What one expects and intends also makes a difference, so *you actually feel more weary in the third lap of a mile than the fourth.*

You don't take out a magnifying glass for what you can see with the naked eye, nor a codebook to read plain English, so when and how can we bring on our amplifiers? Exceptional situations must surely justify some kind of exceptional approach. *Once you suspect that this innocent postcard might be the secret message of a spy, you muster extra power to decode it.*

For people without exceptional curiosity, many secrets and enigmas, many details and patterns are left unnoticed. I find that creative people actually see more problems than others do. They not only spot some gap between what should be and what is actually happening, they also seek what might happen in the future and what they might do to avoid it or make it happen. They create a gap, either through wishing to raise standards, or in a kind of restless discontent. Hope provides the energy, both to create the gap and then to close it with some improvement.

Creative people look farther, wider and more frequently. Motivation is another feature: some people are more likely to be satisfied with the

71

instructions programmed for them, whilst the unusual achiever keeps trying to transcend, overcome or explore beyond—in short, to determine his own directions, to find a better way. The steeper the barriers, the greater his ingenuity in rising above them. Man's creative drive is built in, and the best of us can release it without straining too hard. That secret lies somewhere within the harmony and integration of body, mind and spirit. Once found, it seems to come naturally. In the next few chapters I will focus on how to look for it and bring it up to best use.

Chapter 6
Perception: Not What it Seems

Reality comes in two forms: what exists or happens and what a person registers in his mind. Both are true, but different, and the subjective impression can often be on top – without the person realising this. Much of our knowledge and skill is tacit, so it's hard to recognise an illusion, harder still to feel our own bias. But all this offers opportunity to come up with ideas that are quite different from our current perceptions.

1. Perception: the way I see the world

*"To be is to be perceived… If a tree falls in a forest and
no one is around to hear it, does it make a sound?"*
BISHOP BERKELEY

All my life, I have been building a more and more complex and subtle architecture in my mind from how I have perceived experiences and events, what I have done and what's happened to me. This 'world-view' comes through all my senses, in whatever 'language' I receive it, and includes my values, wishes, hopes and fears, the reasons why some things appeal and others are distasteful. Moreover it affects what I think will probably happen, how things are related to one another, and so on. All these together combine to make 'Perception.' These subjective impressions can become stronger than the objective reality out there, and they may last a lifetime.

The beauty of these unconscious images is that they are so inconsistent and unreliable that they offer a magnificent source of new and original ideas, which by definition do not conform to any stable raft of knowledge and judgment. *"If you cannot change your mind, you cannot change anything"* (George Bernard Shaw).

Truth comes on different levels and Wittgenstein reminds us that if someone thinks you are a liar, then that is true, even when you're not. We widen or narrow our scope according to whether we consider the issue from a high, general and all-embracing perspective, or whether from a lower, more specific and immediate viewpoint: should I try to change the world or begin with myself? At times, what one says today is an attempt to counterweight what one said last week—but the person listening might not realize that, nor even the speaker. In fact it's rare to think things through properly: "I've never had a Guinness because I don't like it" ran the famous beer advertisement. And does 'aggressive' mean something bad or good? In America, at last count there were more than a dozen famous financial funds with 'Aggressive' in their title. How appealing is that?

When I listen to a particular sound, what I hear is affected by other sounds, close by, far off, heard before and even after; I can block out the 'music' from the nearby apartment by playing something I prefer, or I can change the situation by singing along to it. But this is nothing compared with the influence of all the memories in my mind since I was small, the values that have accrued which make that apartment's music alien or distasteful. Time shrinks or expands, just like space, which differs according to our viewing point, where we are when we observe it, and also from our point of view or opinions. If a cylinder presents itself one way, it is a circle, if another, a rectangle. The nut tightens on a bolt clockwise, though when looking from above when tightening from below, the person sees it as anti-clockwise. Moreover, the phenomenon applies to all sense perceptions. Whatever we look at is seen differently according to its situation and background and according to the state of the observer. A wave or a particle can be the same thing, in a different state, just as a person can be a pedestrian or a motorist. Recently, noise pollution from wind turbines has been found so serious that they are actually adding the sound of rustling leaves, to alleviate the harmful effects. Electric motorcars were at first too quiet for pedestrian safety.

Relativity rules, OK? "You put your mind in exact accordance with things as they really are," said James Clerk Maxwell, who brought together electricity, magnetism and light as three phenomena of the same thing. This is actually impossible, unless you say he aimed to do so. Looking in the mirror, which is really your right ear? So don't try using a mirror to tie your bow tie! Emily at 14 sees time differently now from how she will when she's 28, and from her 50 year old mother, or from her grandfather. "Images, then, begin to look like our way of representing significance to ourselves" (Mary Warnock). Does something matter because I want to deal with it (subjective) or because it needs to be dealt with (objective)?

Philosophers have explored this phenomenon of suspect perception for centuries: we get the wrong picture in many ways, or fail to get the full picture. What I think I experienced is almost as likely to be wrong as what I predict will happen in the future. Whatever is 'observed' can be treated as an 'event between' the object and the observer, just as teaching and learning are each events between teacher and learner. So-called 'child-centered learning' is absurd.

Figure 6.1. my Rorschach image

What do you think this is? There are many answers, all true. It is not your eyeball that sees the image above, but the brain behind your eye. So what we experience may not be 'what is there' but rather our response to it. Some resonance occurs between the outside world and our inner interpretation. Actually I made the image from folding the page over a blob of ink. It changes as the person changes. 'She cannot dip her foot in the same river again' because the river has flowed on since last year and so has she.

Every week the advances of science discover that some aspect of yesterday's medical advice is not quite true. Every day, people observe an illusion. That huge harvest moon just above the horizon is not a few hundred yards away; the sky on a wintry morning is not so dark as it looks—you only have to turn off the lights in the bedroom. It is not at all obvious that the earth goes round the sun, and I was extremely confused when first in Cape Town, that the sun travelled from right to left from sunrise to sunset! We are thus gulled innocently into acceptance of what is apparently happening, what seems to be so. But this has the advantage of affording human beings an infinite capacity for making our own personal interpretations of whatever we experience. Where is north? Or 'soon'? How far is it to the nearest inn—miles or minutes? Could we store light and if so, how? Any connection with storing heat in steam, or energy in a spring? What is the distance between just short of infinity and just beyond it?

The Law, Accountancy and Science either purposefully exclude some kinds of information as if they cannot be relied upon, or they handle information (such as money) as if only such professionals can. What are we to make of this quote from the Financial Times? "Since 1900, equities have historically produced 5.3% a year." They subtract pounds sterling spent in one year from pounds sterling in another, or gaily compare house prices here and in the United States using the dollar exchange rate. Gold is real, money virtual? People commonly assign more 'hard relevance' to the words than the music behind them; and again more to numbers than mere words. Perhaps one can see drawing as more intellectual, painting more emotional. Maybe, the bias of would-be scientists against subjective information could account for their vulnerability to the phenomenon known as 'invincible ignorance.' (Really good scientists know better.)

The novelist Sebastian Faulks said in a radio interview in 2009 that when his wife visited his office, where he did all his writing, she had never before been so aware of how much of his life was 'away.' They had been happily married for years and of course writing and living life, like perceptions and reality, do not often coincide perfectly!

2. Much of our knowledge is tacit

"The greater portion of our total mental activity goes on outside conscious awareness" (Stanford Research Institute 1985). When thinking is autonomic, it acts as an unfelt constraint, making awareness essential.

Subliminal impressions and memories sometimes form our most important influences (see *The Tacit Dimension* by Michael Polanyi). We are not aware of the differences between liking a thing and wanting it; between what we need and what we want; between pleasure and happiness, between what we would like as much as possible of and what we must have for our goal to be viable. All these pairs are far from identical! Duncan Bannatyne, the millionaire Scot of "Dragons' Den," might refuse to invest in the would-be entrepreneur's company, yet actually buy its product. When a person wants to convey something to someone else, neither party troubles to think what it might mean to the other. We focus on the apparent, ignoring what is significant by its absence, with often-fatal results. As Nonaka and Takeuchi described in *The Knowledge Creating Company*, some of an expert's skill is hidden from him—he doesn't really know how he does it or why it works: memorably, in researching for a breadmaking machine, the top baker in Japan was unaware of a critical twist he always gives the dough—which had to be imparted in the design. When a local person gives directions to a stranger, he or she often leaves out some details critical to the stranger, but all too well known to the local resident. "Turn left a mile before you reach the pub." How do you tell a townsman how to get a log fire going well—tell him how to do it badly as well? The Spanish proverb warns to take great care over what you pray for—your prayers might be answered; just as your computer might actually do what you tell it to do, not what you really intended! This 'tacit knowledge' is hard to challenge, just because we don't know we hold it, so that these silent impressions become more in charge of us than we are in charge of them.

Misunderstandings are so often bewildering because the assumptions made are not valid. "People who can repeat what you are saying are not listening" (Hugh Kingsmill). In the UK, I wonder how many voters realize that 40% taxpayers must earn 167% of the cost of anything they wish to purchase. Or whether a 50% markup is more of a bargain than a 33% discount.

3. Illusion

What we see exists? Doubting Thomas had to press his fingers into the wounds of the crucified Christ before he could commit, and it's hard to get anyone to believe that when s/he meets with resistance, it is not there.

Images are indeed abstract, yet they pack a punch. We choose whether to say one quarter or twenty-five percent or the actual amount, sometimes with care. Words often have connotations that might not be consistent. Which way is 'Up'—does it mean north or good? Is Up always better than Down? Does basic mean elementary or profound, strategic, or at a high level of abstraction—the Latin word *altus* (for altitude) means both deep and high. In a flowchart of thought and actions, should time go from left to right, top down or bottom up? Is a headline in the newspaper less or more true than its text in smaller font?

4. Values: what is 'good'?

It is values that make an idea worth entertaining. Few people really know what their values are, so they need expression, even for their owner. So it's useful to see 'creativeness' in the <u>approach</u> of the person concerned, rather than simply in the unique originality of any idea itself. "There are two experiences, an inward or imaginative one called seeing, and an outward or bodily one called painting, which in the painter are inseparable" (R G Collingwood). Emotions certainly affect what we 'hear' or receive, which makes politics so notorious. The fact is, people one thoroughly disapproves of are trying to make decisions that are 'right'—whoever wants to make the wrong one?—and this must surely be the highest-level intention shared by the whole of humanity. Claiming the Government is doing the 'right' thing is mere rhetoric. All depends on what works and on one's values and perceptions, and these influence each other. Moreover, we change our opinions, our needs and our wants, so the fashion icon of one year is old hat the next.

The hardest thing is to want what we need. As the old farmer said to the young official from the Ministry of Agriculture, "Look, sonny, I already know how to farm better than I do," but he cherished independence. People will carry on smoking or even take it up, they drink too much at a time and too often, they consume dangerous additives and recklessly eat junk food and take drugs, "Because it's nice!" Ultimately, we always make up our own mind, even when this entails self-denial and altruism. Do not ever be kind to a masochist!

5. Awareness puts us in control

"I am someone to whom this feeling belongs, not something belonging to it."

R G Collingwood is very clear: "The watching of his own work with a vigilant and discriminating eye which decides at every moment of the process whether it is being successful or not, is not a critical activity subsequent to and reflective upon the artistic work, it is an integral part of that work itself." Compare this with Cecil Day Lewis, poet, saying, "We write in order to understand, not to be understood."

Thoughts are the result of abstraction, virtual action inside the mind, which is so fluid. Turning them into real action in the world outside slows you down and if we had to spell out what we were struggling with, we could not go fast enough to hold the emerging thought together. So original thinking often begins fuzzy and incoherent, in some sort of Cloud of Unknowing (from a 14th century English mystic). This is why we have so much recourse to symbolic language, which includes drawing and waving our hands about! Imagination exists to conjure out of the air anything not yet apparent, as with Plato's 'abstract forms.' Things do exist and events do happen, whether or not one witnesses them. There are known knowns. These are things we know that we know. "There are known unknowns. That is to say, there are things that we know we don't know. But there are also unknown unknowns. There are things we don't know we don't know". (Donald Rumsfeld, former US Secretary of Defense)

6. Measurement

"You can only make as well as you can measure"
JOSEPH WHITWORTH

Every skill, every arena of human activity develops its own terms or special vocabulary, which acts like a kind of currency to make trading in thought possible. Size is an important aspect of any image formed: scale matters. So we developed a 'language' for measurement. As soon as we could measure reliably, we could count on building the Pyramids. Mendel's work improved botany; Mendelev developed his table of elements to bring greater accuracy to chemistry; cracking DNA has already accelerated our understanding of human biology, even if it appears to see little difference between a human and a banana or a fruit-fly! What scale to measure with depends on the image we form of our purpose, so key parameters are how big or small, how many and how connected.

- Nano-technology is working in billionths of a meter, or about 50,000 times finer than a human hair. This means perhaps five atoms side by side or the width of a single strand of DNA. Manipulating atoms and molecules on this scale is so unfamiliar, but it makes possible entirely new material substances, such as graphene.

- Some people fear that working on some materials at this level will be so insidious as to be hard to control; perhaps worse than asbestos particles, germ warfare, poison gas.
- The fumes from the green paint on his walls were said to have done for Napoleon at St Helena.
- Who would have thought that weather or rain could be influenced by bubbles or the population of microbes in the clouds?
- And now the particle accelerator at CERN has found the Higgs boson.

Of course there is more than smallness at work there, not least the physical properties. Yet the smaller the point of a needle, the sharper, and the easier it will penetrate. And where would agriculture be without those trillions of little beasties working away in the soil?

There are three factors to consider: size, number and connection.

a) **Size: how big or small.** What these examples have in common is being tiny and unnoticeable. What you cannot see, you fear—unless of course you ignore it altogether, and by contrast, we also tend to ignore things so large we cannot comprehend them. How huge are the distances in astrophysics, how many universes do you say there are? Sometimes, subjective 'feel' over-rules objective measurement. *A perfect square on the page doesn't look quite square enough.* Loudness of sound is not heard just in decibels and frequencies.

Indeed it is notable how these days we bandy about huge numbers such as terabytes and more, with very little real grasp of their relative size. Consider how planet Earth becomes a smaller and smaller pinpoint when compared with the sun, and all the successive systems and galaxies of the total universe. Compare the 14 billion years since the big bang with the acceleration in its first second—you can hardly begin. It's a revelation to discover how long it takes to count a million one-dollar banknotes—nearly eight weeks of 35 hours at one per second! So when Royal Bank of Scotland makes a loss of 28 billion pounds in the year 2008, counting it would take more than a year's work for over 4300 bank clerks! Must be boring! To comprehend such enormity requires either visual display or (literally) imagination.

Our language of analogy for size may conflict with another scale. Older people used to inches may still find it hard to picture millimeters, Celsius when used to Fahrenheit and so on. Hands (for horses), cubits, yards, chains and miles (1000 paces of the Roman soldier) are so much more user-friendly. Those original analog measurements relate to Man and his subjective perceptions, whereas the metric system is objective. On two huge projects I know of, NASA failed to recognize the metric system, with disastrous results in space. No wonder the USA has no plan to convert, even to international paper sizes!

b) Number: how many. There is nothing in the known universe more complex than this mind of ours. Yet, the ordinary voter faced with government figures in billions cannot cope because s/he cannot form a 'real' image of them. "If we considered the number of possible neural circuits, we would be dealing with hyper astronomical numbers: 10, followed by at least a million zeros. (There are 10 followed by 79 zeros, give or take a few, of particles in the known universe.)" (Edelman and Tononi, *Consciousness*) There is also a lot more 'space,' and how do you count whatever may be outside space? What about the one million billion connections or synapses we command? We need a user-friendly human scale. In fact "the magical number 7 ± 2" is as much as most people can handle at once!

c) Connections. No one would deny that the complexity of the physical universe places ever-increasing demands on science to plumb the depths of how the world works. It's the task of interpreting the myriad relationships influencing one another. When I was a child, I was told that the atom was the smallest thing there was—and now look at its complex infrastructure, and the universe of laws and motion inside each one. As much could be said of the philosophical universe... In both cases, it is not adequate (though essential) to rely purely on logic and accurate, definable data. Things we cannot box or cut up have to be imaged, so since we acquired Indian/Arabic numerals, calculation has been so much easier and faster. In fact any numbering system itself makes comprehension easier by chunking into dozens, scores, sixties, or hundreds, thousands, millions, billions, trillions... So we can reduce escalating numbers to 5K or 17m or 12bn etc., as if there were still only a manageable few.

Finally, we work with all sorts of scales, measures or formulae, and their counterparts in aesthetics are the abstract conventions of art. Music is essentially made up of images in sound that carry profound meaning. At its simplest is the song. How could you put the tune of one kind of song to the words of another? The result is so incongruous that on the BBC radio show "I'm Sorry I Haven't a Clue," the panelists are forced to do just that—which is very funny. At the other end of the scale, opera is considered one of the highest forms of art. Yet because the actual words sung can barely be followed, the story is conveyed through acting and then almost entirely by the images created by the composer and his musicians.

I hope that these various examples make it plain how imagery is not only the result of thinking in a less-usual way, but also the stimulus for thinking up ideas in the first place. Once aware of our spontaneous images, we can generate <u>new</u> ideas by violating them!

Chapter 7
The Language of Imagery

Images reflect personal impressions and are like words of extraordinary versatility, so they offer a language for thinking with infinite scope. The impressions they reflect are less tangible and exacting than words or numbers, yet this elusive nature allows unusual connections to be reached without any proper rational pathways. Pictures in the mind work faster, deeper and wider, more simply than precision naming. They bring a special order and coherence, so vital to make ideas that work, especially when shared with others. Like metaphor, they supply 'the music behind the words' and it's often the space between or around something that is more important in making a vital connection.

1. Images are flexible thought-buckets

Pictures are better on radio than television: we are forming them ourselves. The word 'imagination' is described in one dictionary (Collins) as 'the faculty or action of producing mental images of what is not present or has not been experienced.' So it is whatever <u>makes</u> images in one's mind. But there always is a connection between the known and the novel idea, bridging your sensing with intelligible thought (Warnock). The images form as icons in our mind, acting as the currency for recognizing the thoughts in our unformed mental groping. I have worked with people who say that science demands that everyone use one word and one word only, to express the same thing. In the humanities, this is almost a crime of repetition. One should have said one <u>term</u> only!

Language describes some core characteristic shared by all the other things of the same name. To distinguish one experience from another, we nail those images in our memory, capturing them as portable 'thought-buckets' that can be used again and again. Picking grapes in bunches is easier and less work than picking and carrying them one at a time. You put bunches together, making bunches of bunches in a basket, then into the cart, and so on. Categories form a reusable container to carry all their items together in one go, offering speed, economy and greater reach. So words are names and symbols that stand for whole classes of similar items and actions. *Is a tomato fruit or vegetable? Is a porpoise a fish?* How shocking to us now that early settlers in Tasmania pictured the aborigines as not quite human, and therefore could be hunted down. Yet how could we live socially without stereotyping people? Seeing someone for the first time, we instantly form an identikit, enabling us to recognize him or her on the next occasion: our image had better convey what is true about them.

As the pre-eminent human activity, thinking itself can be described as the manipulation of images in the mind, as distinct from doing things physically out in the real world. It is a kind of rehearsal or simulation, acting at a distance, fast and economical.

Making the ephemeral tangible

The rough image that appears in our mind as a new idea has to be made more material, so as to shape it into something useful and real. In spite of Descartes' great work, we can go too far in separating the mind from the body, though there are still some medical people who use the word 'psycho-somatic' for a delusional illness, as if they had not yet realized that most physical illness is affected by what's working in the patient's mind. Even doctors can fail to realize the useful implications of 'placebos,' and a patient is able to both alleviate and make worse the effects of some external invasion of the body, or even bring it on. At last, the profession is coming to the curative value of metaphors created in or by the patient. Star athletes and their coaches are keenly aware of the symbiotic relationship constantly flowing between body and mind. At peak moments, it is the mind that determines whether or not you win the race, as confessed by David Hemery, Olympic gold-medal winner, who narrowly failed in his second Games. For it to happen on the day, the high jumper must envision his successful leap. I heard recently of a young English snowboarder, competing in the Alps against the world's best, with no sponsorship, and for whom access to snow was out of the question most of the year. Yet without going anywhere, using hours of footage on the web, he could visualize tricks in his head for aerobatics on steep slopes, using neither snow nor board. Thinking, mostly in images, is what forms the bridge or connection between the person inside and the world outside him. We become conscious when we infuse that connection with intention, the aiming or direction of our thought processes. Only when more conscious of those myriad shapes and subtleties do we effectively exercise our free will. The goalkeeper has to second-guess the intention of the scorer so as to dive the right way.

Figure 7.1. Scoring your goal

All forms of information experienced, all sensations, are themselves impressions, some form of image. Years ago in the House of Commons, Jennie Lee was harassed by an opposing member who said, "Why don't you think before you open your mouth?" In robust indignation she replied, "*How can I know what I think until I have said it?*" Thinking up an idea leads to finding how to put it in some usable form. Doing that stimulates a further new idea, as in when writing poetry, the rhyme required forces you to think what to write before it.

All the muses use images, usually formed before the idea can be put into words or number. Art is so often a harbinger of change in society or trend, as when the height of the hemline predicts the economy! The eye of the mind 'sees' the 'ideon,' the spirit of truth, the essence of 'else,' the soul of 'otherness.' Plato saw eyes as "windows of the soul" and Queen Elizabeth I followed him. Sketches are like the fleeting phrases captured when composing music, the instant gesture of the choreographer and the unposed movement the photographer would hope for.

2. The picturing of memory and experience

When I first presented my innovative work to Professor Rom Harre at the Department of the Philosophy of Science at Oxford, one of the books it spurred him to suggest was *The Art of Memory* by Frances Yates. He clearly had made a connection.

All experience is retained in the memory in the form of symbols, some of which are words. The nature of images is to represent many meanings at once and in various ways, some implicitly, others explicitly. We can use the word 'hot' on a scale from temperature to mustard, to orange as against blue, to passion, to hot music or news, and ultimately, in *Some Like It Hot*, to Marilyn Monroe—or to Brigitte Bardot if you prefer. One can tolerate hearing a fine piece of music through a really bad recording or radio station, listening with the mind's ear and purposely ignoring the awful quality of sound. We can enjoy even karaoke, or gathering round the piano in a pub, 'experiencing' the real beauty of the original music. In every field, we thus compensate for our senses, recognizing the invalidity of what they tell us; a table should appear square only from directly above, but when we see it from any other 'normal' position, we correct for the angle of observation. The spirit commonly over-rides the letter of the law.

How one represents an insight is tinged or flavored with what's already present in one's memory vault. Some people 'get it' in sound, which has its own architecture and structure for meaning; smell, the earliest sense in Man, and taste are more elusive, so they are typically represented by analogy, as in the wine charts that describe the range of tones and flavors of comparable fruits. No wonder the language for ideas is seen as 'imagery,' and hence imagination.

Although fleeting, the first harbingers of something new may come from memories put together in a different way. They include our emotions and feelings, our values and beliefs, held in the brain or somehow in the blood-stream, our limbic system, our bodily chemistry, 'in our bones.' *Even grass 'remembers' it was trodden down earlier.* They seem always ready to hand, we never have to rack our brains for them: like instincts, they are almost impossible to forget and are immediate. As soon as you try to remember anything, it shows as a picture in your mind, whether literally visual or from other senses. If ever I encounter rancid butter, my mind flashes back to an afternoon tea at school when I was just eight years old. When I cannot recall an experience, I am failing to match what I want it for with the one I stored in a memory that is always on the move. Yet brilliant new ideas may well be drawn from that rich seed-bed—but compared, altered, opposed, exploited, expanded, explored and taken into new realms.

In practical terms, the capitalized value of the company itself can be worth less than its 'brand.' A board of directors may find it very difficult to formulate a new strategy because it's so hard to capture the very nature, the spirit of their whole business. They need that so as to envision what they would like the company to achieve and become. Both these tasks are best done physically, by sketching pictures, by making models, through music, even by mime and drama. The actual, material arrangement of shapes and colors, texture and light helps them catch the abstract 'message' of their picture. Treating a concept as something spatial and physical where it can literally be 'handled' with the hand helps it to be connected with almost anything, however abstract, such as the almost ethereal love that joins mother and child.

Figure 7.2. The feeling within (Cecil William Rhodes)

3. Language takes many forms

A new invention is often the result of applying a different technology to the subject's natural one. (That's what jokes often do!) In 1940, when Britain was under severe threat of invasion and defeat, desperate measures were called for. Churchill asked for leading figures in entirely diverse disciplines to be pulled together into a kind of 'think-tank,' in the belief their differences could be synthesized into inventing extraordinary weapons to win the war. Now we know they often succeeded, but then it was an outlandish notion to put an archaeologist and a physicist and a mathematician and a musician together. Yet out of this initiative was born the new multi-disciplinary science we call OR, Operations Research. Thinking is naturally multi-disciplinary and this enables top executives to govern the business without being expert in the knowledge required, so long as they can rely on good processes. This is still an outrageous idea apparently: when the head of Her Majesty's Revenue and Customs declared she was not a tax expert, she evoked much laughter and was all over the papers next day. Even so, information systems are designed to be the 'central nervous system' of the organization, doing the thinking for and on behalf of their users.

Physics is today adding insight in biology and medicine and it is now common to cross the frontiers of the five senses, enabling us to show sound visually as voiceprints that discriminate as accurately as the fingerprints of Alphonse Bertillon (biography by Henry T F Rhodes). In the same way, heat can be photographed and mapped, and by applying different sets of 'rules' infrared enables us to see in the dark and detect forgeries by 'seeing' the difference in inks. Some cancers may be foiled by ultra-sonics.

For communicating, we usually turn to words, but actually images are often better, simpler, faster, deeper and wider. "Let pictures be as poems" wrote Horace. "In ancient Egypt, when literacy was a restricted skill, pictures were more significant than words" (A C Grayling on The Book of the Dead). Language itself has a subtle role to play in noticing, remembering, judging and changing into something original. Is it reason or imagination that recognizes the tune in musical sounds? Perhaps it is when both functions are in harmony that we experience that feeling of 'beauty,' which gives satisfaction equally in art and in science. Nobody suggests that words are closer to science than pictures and it is hard to do art or science without some visual imaging. The choral music of John Dunstable, from the 15th century, has been described as 'cathedrals of sound.'

Jargon is invariably vilified when used in the company of people not 'in the know,' but this language is an essential element in anyone's effectiveness, so professionals have names for all the specialist things they deal with. Whenever you engage in some new field, at first you feel unable to do much because you don't know the lingo. In the Bible story of genesis, it was the art of naming everything in creation that was the great gift from God to Adam and Eve, as they went out into the world. Naming signaled the dawn of the awareness given to mankind, and the development of all knowledge in every single field, whether art or science, has depended on it ever since. Each culture has grown, by heuristics and in parallel, its languages of symbols and semantics, grammar and syntax. I say symbols because, as you know, language embraces all the arts and senses and physical activities, all the domains of science and mathematics. I am told that *singing originated to express and convey emotions*, before there was 'language' in words. However, it seems we applied it first to all the concrete things we met and made in the world, and much later to the more abstract and invisible workings of our inner mind.

These attempts to capture the complexity in simple form are vital to ideas, which run like mercury all over the place and can all too easily disappear.

Above all, language makes coherence. It is more than vocabulary, but, rather, a system for putting concepts together in various permutations or configurations, to convey a variety of different meanings. The language of the Inuit in Northern Canada has few words, but multiple connections between them. A special type of snow is called 'snow for building igloos with' and for obvious reasons the same word, 'shak,' can also be used for plywood. Other languages with few words, for instance African or Maori, have many tones and nuances to multiply their usefulness. Even English, which is rich in words, has similar tricks: try all the ways you can possibly say the words of the song title "What Now My Love?" or savor the TV advertisement "Is That Your Car?" Only the tone of voice or demeanor assures you get the right message, when the words in cold print cannot ever be sure of avoiding huge misunderstandings!

Language is clearly for more than the <u>expression</u> of thoughts to someone else; it is also for communicating with oneself, that is, thinking. The art critic Philip Hensher declared, "For most artists, drawing is a way of thinking on paper." Engineers and architects too are continually forming patterns of some kind, and expression throws light on their workings, and helps to reach out for new thoughts or to connect with old ones.

In singing, meaning entails the explicit encoding of the sounds and the implicit imagery around the notes. The Anglo-Saxon language of neumes made up a notational system of signs which showed the direction of the melody being sung and some detail of expressiveness—but apparently not the precise pitch. Now we have amazingly complex musical scores, gathering together what has to be played by perhaps an orchestra of 100 instruments, all at once. Even the written guidance of how it should feel is then interpreted—quite variously—by each famous conductor! His body language in rehearsals may use all kinds of vocal directions, not even singing and sometimes of extraordinary crudity, to get his orchestra to play the score in particular ways: his expressive grunts and noises are getting at the flavor of the piece, its essential spirit. The layman amateur, when humming or whistling the tune, also captures the spirit of the piece, even when he makes a few mistakes, and he gets pleasure from his efforts, even if his roommates might not!

Hearing a tune, watching a dancer, visiting an exhibition of an artist unknown to us, we always abstract from the experience some image, differentiating it from all others. Until you label, write, or draw something, you cannot relate it to other labeled things or move it from one place to another or see any causal connection through time or space that captures meaning. So we formulate images too, a signature, a logo, a rule or law, and so on. Whether one feels this is rationally making out what is there or inventively making it up depends mostly on your intention at the moment.

The formulae of algebra and geometry and chemistry present yet another kind of language explicitly encoded in images, and as for mathematical or chemical <u>concepts</u> we would be severely limited without all the symbols of quantity and quality which they live on.

Protagoras (b. 490 BC) wrote, "Man is the measure of all things." Two thousand years later, Leonardo da Vinci (1490) made this iconic drawing of Vitruvian Man. The words added within his picture are of course mine!

Figure 7.3. Vitruvian Man—after Leonardo da Vinci

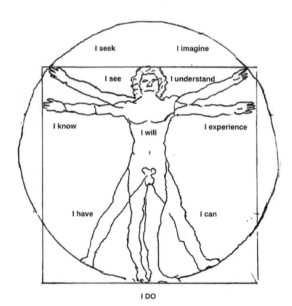

4. Metaphor, the ultimate connector

"In the beginning was the Word, and the Word was with God," and the word is Metaphor. Using one word literally may well create a joke. "When I use a word," Humpty Dumpty said in rather a scornful tone, "it means just what I choose it to mean—neither more nor less" (Lewis Carroll, *Through the Looking-Glass…*). Words nearly always have several meanings, making often-remote connections between experiences familiar to the public but now revealed in a different light. We speak of the sword of truth, the shield of justice or arrows of imagination or desire! No wonder art is subject to so many quite different interpretations.

Figure 7.4. Cupid's bow (Cecil William Rhodes)

There is no end to the images and connections you can make. It's as if your inner world of memory is like a giant universe, starred with millions of pictures in which you travel so much faster than the speed of light that you are timeless. You can link your stars with silken ropes in countless directions to form new pathways in your mind. New images are thus born, new configurations in your world, new perceptions of conceivable reality. Such things are art works in the mind, imagination. 'Image' is used in psychology to represent 'something not immediately present to the senses.' Sight is transformed through intuition into insight, so we commonly say 'I see' when meaning 'I understand.'

Douglas Hofstadter, the cognitive scientist who wrote *Gödel, Escher, Bach*, declared in an interview with *New Scientist* in October 2005 that, "Making analogies is central to being human. Every single word choice we make is done by analogy." Choosing whether to say 'Middle Ages' or 'medieval' might seem trivial, but for a computer it would be terribly hard to handle, unless it had been programmed to understand the connotations. These veer wildly, according to one's appreciation of Christendom and how advanced and civilized were the Middle Ages. The words we choose connect to more and more abstract levels until we build up very deep insights (or delusions) about reality.

There are numbers that feel more soft, feminine and non-confronting, and so are used in Marketing when it comes to establishing (low-seeming) prices. Some colors are seen as masculine or feminine, and others as up-market or down-market. When GKN founded a subsidiary company to market central heating to the less-well-off general public, its livery and style of advertising and brochures were firmly changed from what had suited its prestigious history and reputation. *It now went for orange!* Solid sculpture can show life and movement, whilst a painter can make an eye sparkle, and a smile to show the subject is concealing thoughts. *What makes a line lively, or a lively line?* Of course, there are millions of such examples of the implicit, yet such phenomena hint at the value of penetrating imagery. The mind has often been likened to an iceberg, with the unconscious beneath the surface many times the size and importance of the conscious. On the other hand, it is by becoming conscious that we increase our chances to aim and steer this huge imponderable force, and symbolic imagery is "the major route between the conscious and the unconscious" (Fechner). A century elapsed between Jenner's vaccination and Pasteur's inoculation, simply because the shared principle for securing immunization was not connected.

Successful imagery, whether analogy, metaphor, fable, simile, parable or allegory, draws upon experience which is similar in essence to the subject being explored—but different enough to heighten awareness or provide a new perspective. Similes and examples represent ideas in tangible, concrete form, and strange enough to suggest further associations more readily. "Only connect." (E M Forster). The image that works has captured an otherwise-obscure characteristic shared by the two different situations, producing the insight required, when we could have looked in vain at the original. A famous Iraqi poet, whose verses were circulated hand to hand everywhere in support of bringing down the tyrant Saddam Hussein, says, "If you speak in a direct way, it does not affect the people." Imagery quickens interest and engages appeal by capturing this spirit of meaning. It helps people to understand the idea and catch on: a parable succeeds partly because of its apparent irrelevance or remoteness, so that the listener is gulled to go along with it freely, only to find it closes on its objective from a surprising angle. No doubt this is why Jesus Christ made so many parables, and the device is common among other great teachers.

Kandinsky was clear that line, color and form could show abstract ideas, and in management education programs I do this in my tools for mapping thought. I believe that thought can sometimes best be represented spatially, and I encourage the use of visuals to join data offered by the senses and the process of the intellect. The pentagon also forms the basis for a great many triangles, when joining the dots in a variety of directions:

Figure 7.5 a pentagon of triangles

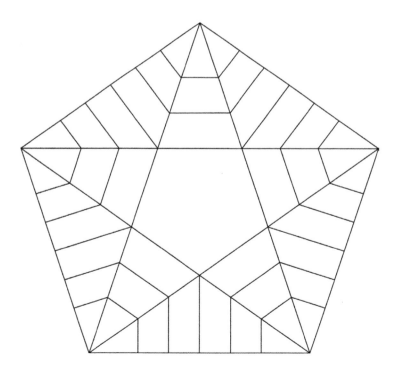

When a geologist or paleontologist discovers a goodly number of fossils/specimens of some as yet unknown creature, he can deduce a reasonably accurate model of what it looked like by laying all the images on top of one another. Imagination does this without such physical arranging.

True originality may have to start where language ends, words being mere vehicles for their thought-passengers, for it is the thoughts that matter. Rational thought, step by step at the speed of words, is rather slow, whilst thinking in symbols can fly faster from one peak to another, as if logical gravity were not there. Reason follows strong rules that get in the way of free expression, so symbol and metaphor give you a short cut, which transcends or leaps beyond the mechanisms and constraints of a rule.

5. The arts

The arts are seen by many as the height of creativity, but I prefer to recognize how they are found in such a wide range of achievements that it's worth separating the expression of beauty in a special way from the conceiving of an original idea. One has to go beyond mere novelty to create something new that works and adds value to those who embrace it. Nonetheless, the enormous range of the arts sends beams of light upon many ways we could all exploit our imaginative faculties.

Aesthetics is really about seeking the truth that lies in beauty. It tries to act as a bridge between conceptualizing an idea and understanding it well enough to respond. It heightens our experience by giving such an intense quality of unity and excitement in the here and now that we speak of 'knowing' it. It has happened to us, taken possession of us, and this brings some kind of ownership and power: at the root of the word 'know' is that 'I can.'

Art uses imagery to promote some original view of life that may be tentative or exploratory but will certainly be unusual and personal. This second approach is perhaps closer to the literal meaning of imagination: image-making. It exploits the amazing fluidity of perception as discussed in the previous chapter.

Art of the first kind tries to portray, reflect, or convey through some 'work' a revelation that can reach into the souls of others. This applies not only to physical artifacts such as a poem or a bridge but also to performances such as plays, opera, and, yes, even the latest 'installations.' Arthur Miller, the playwright who wrote many plays directly for US radio, said of Orson Welles, "He understood radio broadcasting better than anyone who ever lived. He would wrap himself round that microphone and come out through the wires." Then it must embrace advertisement, oratory, craft, design and also processes, whether engineering, innovation, persuasion, conversation or even making love!

All these express or 'copy' thought. Perhaps this explains why 'art' is not always 'creative' and may simply be a way of expressing reality; so a portrait can be just a good likeness and still be a good portrait, a landscape can show you what that bay looks like from the sea and a model can show faithfully what the bridge across the English Channel would look like. It need not imply some literal or physical representation: on BBC radio, *the polar bear's footfalls in the snow would not sound authentic if recorded live for radio—so they simulate them 'better' with sound-effects that sound more like footfall than the real thing.*

Unlike a computer, a person does not take in 'facts' and store them in accurate detail, immutably and reliably without question. Instead we form impressions that we can readily recall, and which roughly hold only the essential flavor of what we experienced. But it's the real thing, real to us. This is the strength that we have not (yet) been able to give to our computers, because they have only mere logic—Latin *ratio*, without *intellectus*. When the artist wants to reach further still into a new reality, his work may take on more bizarre form and, like Gerald Scarfe, he may purposefully exploit distortion or exaggeration.

Figure 7.6. the shrewd farm laborer, 1942 (Cecil William Rhodes)

Each one may be 'nothing like the real person' but instantly recognizable, for he has tapped into something profoundly true about his victim. Without mapping onto any of a person's real features, he yet captures the person, what he really does look like and who he really is. Another artist's sketches in the mountains capture the essence of the picture he means to form later in more detail and finesse. It is, by analogy at least, this insight that we all get from our soft imaging which eludes us if we cleave only to hard, quantified and measured aspects of reality. Some time ago, having been doing consulting work for a huge client organization for more than two years, the company lawyer invited me to sign a contract, saying, "I suppose now we must reduce our agreement to writing." Reduce. He had indeed a delicious sense of irony.

Facing up to a blank canvas, one feels the need to put something or other down on its surface at once, else it will stare at one with a deepening sneer— "Can't you decide what to paint on me yet?" One may rough out a wash of color, place a horizon or a couple of verticals; some even prefer to paint over an earlier canvas, and I have more than one portrait my father made, done at the breakfast table on a newspaper! Navigating into the unmapped universe of mind, all you have as "a star to steer you by" is your purpose or goal: what is it you are trying to discover, reach or accomplish? Until you have this vision, you might as well throw paints onto the canvas and walk all over it.

Art sees what is not apparent yet is there, nonetheless; and then it finds extremely unusual ways to execute that vision. Modern British artists have gone far out to deliver what is certainly outrageous to the viewer who was expecting the painting to 'say it how it is': future history will have to determine which works prove to be products of genuine creativity. The portraits by Frank Helmut Auerbach (born 1931) may at first appear strange, due to his individually expressionist style, yet each one is instantly recognizable. Through maybe hundreds of sittings and brutal scraping away, he has tapped into something profoundly true about the subject of his portrait. Pablo Picasso could 'draw proper' if he wanted to: he had years of excellent work in his early periods that show this, and in fact is regarded by many artists as a supreme draughtsman. Yet he could paint a woman with her two eyes on one side of the face. Modigliani didn't have to paint people so long and thin, nor Barbara Hepworth make her works so full of holes. The French Impressionist Edgar Degas (1834–1917) saw ballet itself as a form of language. "I'm not a painter of dancers, but I'm trying to find movement." Those contortions may be more lasting and bring more value than 'conventional' images though it is not only modern art that reveals some new reality in what most of us see.

Figure 7.7. Dancers (Cecil William Rhodes)

In a way, all examples of art are 'Impressionist' and it is a matter of how best to make an impression on the audience. Is it what you <u>put in</u> to the picture or what you <u>leave out</u>? A Cold bias might insist on all the accuracy and details being in a portrait, while a Warm bias might convey the nature of the person more by suggestion than by outline. A few strokes of the designer's pen can say more about the nature of the new product concept than an accurate model; in some of the world's greatest works, the main thing is the powerful and lasting impression you receive. The nature of the engineering exploded diagram differs from a drawing or a photograph, because their purposes are different, and in a presentation an audience will learn more from a rough sketch, drawn live.

The space between things, around and beyond them may be what we fail to see without imagination, and Rachel Whiteread, the English sculptor, has become famous for focusing on this. Silence is golden. What a shame that in these impatient days even the BBC, when making a film, no longer allows the space for those pauses which were so powerful in earlier productions. Interruptions of nothing have value. They will come back.

There are those who do not yet see photography as 'art,' but it has always been more than a technical affair. Herman Leonard, who died in 2010, worked under Karsh in Ottawa after the war, and photographed many of the leaders of jazz in the States before publishing *The Eye of Jazz* (1985). He was famous for his black and white pictures of smoke-laden clubs, capturing the essence of the music and the players amid the stink and flavor of their dark surroundings so vividly that "*when people think of jazz, their mental image is most likely one of Herman's photos*" (Quincy Jones). "My principle was to capture the mood…to make people see the way the music sounded," said Leonard. Work like his, in any century, stands primarily for aesthetic description more than the genius of imagination, but everyone sees the creativity in it. Turner's sketches were accurately drawn for pictures that were to be picturesque, romantic, ethereal and appealing compositions.

In the same vein, this imagery runs through and through all of the arts, naturally taking different forms. Dancing, whether in the ballroom or the nightclub, is highly suggestive, and this is taken to its ultimate in Latin American tango and salsa, in the classical ballet of Serge Diaghilev and Nijinsky in Ballets Russes, and the contemporary dance company of Martha Graham. Beautiful imagery in all the muses including sport, architecture, engineering, astro-physics and mathematics is called 'poetry.' Centuries ago, the Chinese identified a language of shape to inform the making of art, so that, for instance, a curving horizontal line sent a signal different from a straight upright one. Goethe and Turner in their paintings adopted colors for warmth (red and yellow) and happiness (green) and foreboding (blue and purple). Whilst different people live with various connotations, these images certainly feel recognizable by many.

Human beings hew out, develop and forge images to serve as a vocabulary for creating and sharing thoughts. Sometimes, we fix their meaning, drawing precise boundary lines, with great clarity. Elsewhere, we take advantage of their fluidity and flexibility to twist and stretch them into new uses, or even to spring to an entirely new idea.

III
Take over your mind

Chapter 8
Turn Barriers into Springboards

Turn those barriers to a new idea into allies, and then take advantage of them. Objections arising from cultural or social backgrounds are usually autonomic and may need more emotional appeal than intellectual argument. Intellectual barriers are easier to confront, knowing that new ideas are bound to conflict with whatever exists. You have to make the rationale for attacking knowledge, structure, probabilities, risk and conformity, in the cause of leaping ahead of standard reason. However new an idea, it will be subjected to enough information and reason to raise anyone's confidence in it.

Whenever you really need a new idea, all the barriers come up. The greatest is how people think—especially yourself! For most people, imagination has not nearly the status of reason, and for the rest, it's easy to feel inhibited. Here we propose that instead of feeling embattled, you embrace these barriers and turn them into springboards for a creative approach.

Figure 8.1. vaulting ingenuity

It is common sense that before committing to any judgment, it is wise to test how sound was the thought process that led you there. You check out the validity of the argument and make sure there are no flaws, faults of reasoning or other factors weakening the case. Like the devil's advocate, whose role is to stop a wrong candidate being made a saint, you throw everything you can at the proposition, to destroy him or her; now you can be more confident of any decision that survives the assault. Conversely, in seeking an original idea, you question every normal judgment made earlier, trying to reverse any unconscious closures made in the past and to start afresh by opening out your mind.

The ideal of disciplined creativity is to possess freedom within rigor within freedom. Switching our stance from passive defense to active attack takes control so as to expand our scope for the exercise of freedom of mind. But, fooling yourself requires not just skill but also motivation. Take someone whose general stance is to feel 'big is good, and bigger better'; what might it take for him to seek something small? What is needed for the American public to embrace using far less energy? Maybe the change itself must be either massive or dramatic, like the Statue of Liberty perfectly crafted by hand within the eye of a needle (yes, it has been done!); perhaps even more of an achievement than the giant faces of those four presidents on Mount Rushmore.

This section is all about attitudes and approach. By exploiting even the deadening processes of the Cool Reasoner, creative skills aim to convert the energy of these negatives into positive insights into your problem which you might never have entertained.

Any new idea, by definition, must necessarily differ from what is already known, and the strange smacks of danger. What is not familiar, outside your ken, activates unconscious reactions which normally protect your survival.

Any barriers to a new idea are best tackled, not avoided. Like assumptions, recognizing them enables you to take advantage of them in all sorts of ways. Every salesman hopes his Prospect will raise their objections, so that he can respond appropriately, not lose the sale. Any good teacher relishes the questions and objections raised by those children in class that bad teachers call 'awkward.' If those nuisance queries don't come, s/he knows they have not 'got it' well enough—or that the child with good questions is ahead already. So the worst thing about barriers is to be unaware of them, or to be unwilling to take them at full punt.

Constraining boundaries and intense competition erect formidable barriers to progress, yet if you make them act like a narrow canyon, that simply speeds up the flow of a river.

The barriers are of four kinds:

Cultural	Physical
Social	Intellectual

They live mostly with the forces in the Stronger Box of Relevance. Really listening to them helps us treat them as friends rather than enemies and especially to harness them in our quest for original ideas. Obstacles become stepping-stones. As in judo, the more powerful the forces against us, the more use we can make of their momentum. So the better we can describe what we know and the more aware we become of the bases for our past and current understandings, the greater is the potential for exploiting them.

Whilst my own experience is very much a part of myself as a person, the more I am prepared to escape from or 'give away,' the more chances I have of achieving the change I need. This requires conscious effort, otherwise people stick with what they know and have done before. This becomes a deadweight, and the worst kind is one carried by others and foisted on you!

1. Cultural barriers

Most ideas have a short life. By definition, a creative idea is out on its own, if only at first. Anyone looking for it has to search where nobody else is, or has ever been. Worse still, the higher the quality of the idea, the farther it will be from the majority of people: it seems a self-defeating recipe. The history of innovation is strewn with the wrecks of ideas that foundered on a hostile reception or environment. Most ideas conceived in some individual's mind are instantly rejected and cast out by that same person, who at once feels his idea to be no good, unworkable or unacceptable by others. "*We have seen the enemy and it is us.*" You won't even try to get it through the opposition if you don't first avoid your own internal barriers. What an irony, suppose the idea would have been a winner! And even today, women still suffer from role stereotyping, such as "Women don't do science, IT, or engineering!" Actually, the history of outstanding women inventors keeps growing, with the emergence of their contributions since the concept of a computer from Ada Byron, Countess of Lovelace, in the early 19th century.

Cultural taboos and beliefs prevent new ideas, whether in the religious or the academic domains. The Not Invented Here (NIH) reaction reflects a culture believing that it can't be any good if 'not from here,' and is extremely widespread in large organizations with a heritage. More ironic is that some such companies actually suffer it twice over: if it's being started somewhere (else) in our organization, it's not for us! It took ten years for an innovation well established in one American business to be accepted by the equally large chunk of the same company on this side of the Atlantic. Now where is Kodak?! Certification of pharmaceutical drugs in one country does not assure acceptance by the National Health Service in Britain. Taboos are buried so far in the past and so deep in our value-system as to arouse no concern whatever. One is about newness or change. The humor in this was beautifully mined some years ago when the governing body of Fellows was debating the status of women in my own college at Oxford. Dacre Balsdon, a wise old tortoise I well remember, declared: "For the past 650 years we have done very well without women undergraduates: whether to admit them should now be considered—over the next 650 years." (I'm glad to say that since then, women students and Fellows have been making an outstanding contribution and the last two heads of Exeter College were Marilyn Butler and Frances Cairncross.)

Only work and duty are worthy. This cultural view is a kind of moral one, born of the so-called Protestant ethic driving much of Northern Europe and the United States. Work, like medicine, should hurt, and short-cut tricks for getting results easily do not deserve to be resorted to. To misquote Thomas Edison, genius <u>ought to</u> be 90% perspiration and only 10% inspiration. Should a big army always defeat a small one, and a heavy book be better than a slim volume on the same subject? I wonder if Einstein's $E = mc^2$ was felt by some to be all too simple… Or "This idea is too ingenious for its own good— it is too close to cheating: not for us." Trying too hard to nail down the right tricks might suffer the risk of seeking the universal solvent: as soon as you think you've found the magic, in what container can you possibly keep it?

2. Social barriers

For imaginative people, ordinary everyday social encounters provide the most obvious and frequent barriers to their inventiveness. In meetings and discussions, in the appraisal of reports and proposals, ideas get squashed.

Lists of killer phrases abound, pointing to the need for any would-be innovator to take care to anticipate objections and be ready with effective response.

We've never done it before
It's not in the budget—we haven't the manpower
We've tried that before—*or* we're not ready for it yet
All right in theory—but can you put it into practice?
What will the customers/parents/suppliers think?
If it were any good, someone would have suggested it before
Too modern—*or* too old hat
Let's discuss this at some better time
You don't understand our problem
We're too small for that—*or* too big
We have too many projects already—not another change/initiative?!
Let's make a market research test first
It has been the same for 20 years, so it must be good
I just know it won't work
Let's form a committee
We'll think it over for a while and watch developments
That's not our problem—*or* it's the responsibility of someone else
Won't work in my territory, department, business
You'll never sell that to top management
Don't move too fast on this
Why something new now?—we're doing well enough
Let's wait until we get the changes at the top completed
Better put it in writing before we go any further
I don't see the connection with…
Political dynamite—*or* it's bound to upset Mr. X
Sounds good, but it's not in the plan
It's too early—*or* too late now
Our people will never accept it
No one outside can tell me how to run my business
Don't for goodness' sake rock the boat now
Etc.…

It's so excusable for the original voice to stop trying, or get lost. No new idea can have any track record: any 'evidence' for it working in real life has to be indirect. Unless he or she makes sure that the evaluation of their idea is well set up, its author may well become easily demotivated.

Here are just three factors that inhibit going out on a limb:

A. Fear, or lack of confidence

Fear of failure, or risking it, has been learned, especially at school and even university, so people normally show caution as a default position. They prefer certainty, or at least a high probability of achieving the desired result, so this limits being flexible. 'Let's use what has usually worked before, even if this situation is a new one.' The unknown is always feared, yet anything already known can hardly be creative or new.

A new idea is often sought when the task seems too ambitious, so you can expect frustration, the feeling that whatever you do is in vain. Naturally this is no fun—unless you are the kind of person that actually enjoys getting around obstacles with ingenuity. Many give up too soon, unwilling to persist in the pursuit of more than the obvious way to deal with an 'impossible' situation.

B. Trust

One can mistrust one's own feelings, especially as they easily lead one astray in the heat of the moment, or overwhelm good sense. When you feel unable or unwilling to deal with conflict, progress is unlikely, because successful resolution depends on it, just as the irritant is needed to produce a pearl. Those who are fertile in ideas revel in the opposition they stir up. Though most strong ideas come from an individual, rather than a group or worse still a committee (!), we do need other people, not only for the diverse experience they bring but as a stimulus and sounding board. When you notice a scowl it doesn't always mean she is mad with you—just wrestling with concentration on a new insight. Warmth and fun are vital fuel for motivation, so make it impossible to take offense in the excitement of idea-reaching. Rather than rely on inter-personal skills, the trick is to openly declare the game being played; to join everyone together in their search for the unusual and then we can leave our normal roles outside the room. Nothing can sour creative effort more sharply than opposition of a personal kind. Since everyone does feel vulnerable sometimes, we must remember that useful opposition is about

What is said, not Who said it. "There is no need to forgive your enemies," said the Dalai Lama. "Rather be grateful to them, for it is from them that you learn."

C. Emotions

Emotion is the source of energy that makes anyone want to do something. Emotions do affect intelligence, just as our intelligence ought to influence and control them. To make good use of emotions is to think.

Figure 8.2. Emotion/intelligence interaction

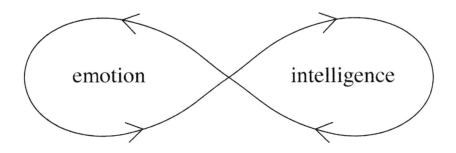

But much of our behavior is unconscious. Our body's chemistry carries all the instincts we have retained in spite of our evolution and they keep driving much of our 'thought-less' behavior. Instincts are physical and act as inhibitors as well as drivers of action. Though we no longer need to worry about the saber-toothed tiger, we suffer fear all right, every day, and a good thing too. It keeps us from doing dangerous things, including adopting ideas that we feel won't work. Even in an apparently civilized discussion, we keep having to choose between fight or flight, and whether the latter could be even more dangerous.

Jordan Peterson, of University of Toronto, says that creative people seem to have brains that are more open to incoming stimuli. The filters we all need for the mass of information assailing us all the time act as what he calls 'latent inhibition,' restricting our receptiveness and also the space in which to juggle a variety of ideas. *Using an electroencephalogram, Colin Martindale from the University of Maine recorded brain wave patterns observed while people made up stories.* At the inspiration stage of dreaming up the stories, the alpha waves were dominant within a very quiet, relaxed mind; perhaps this is why we speak of sleep and dreams as a condition for ideas. When it came to developing their stories, the same people raised their cortical activity, understandably so. *But his significant finding was that those with the biggest time gap between the two phases of inspiration and development produced the most creative storylines.* This supports my own research. Exceptionally creative people are capable of highly logical and convergent as well as wildly divergent thinking. Far better than remaining balanced or neutral, they go out to extremes, rather than remaining lukewarm in the middle of nonentity. S/he drives for wild imagination for all her worth, then pulls in with powerful judgment, then out and in again, with alternating directions, but neither at the expense of the other. *Separate the two approaches in time, lest they nullify each other:* the trick is to be flexible enough to toggle between the two effectively, though the ultimately brilliant ideas often come from their fielding together. Our extensive and longitudinal work on thinking profiles may help explain why. (find more about Rhodes Thinking-Intention Profile at effectiveintelligence..com).

Moreover most people enjoy a natural inertia, a tendency to return to the status quo, to do nothing, to take the line of least resistance. The other face of inertia is that we continue doing what we have been doing before, drawn along by trends. So much so that financial institutions are forced to warn the buyers of shares that they can go down as well as up, and that past performance may not be a reliable indicator of future profits. The game that follows has been given to thousands of managers. *Take a box of matches and lay out three on the table to make a triangle. Then make a second triangle with only two extra. And a third with only seven all told. Now can you make four triangles without the seventh match?* If you try this for a few moments, you will see the point for yourself. There is more than one point of course.

3. Physical barriers

Every person has their own temperament, a built-in inclination or tendency to behave in a particular way because for example s/he is optimistic or pessimistic, passionate or impervious to influence or change. Such preferences do not change, for your temperament derives from the physical body you were born with. You manage them by mental effort, otherwise ideas do not even get conceived, especially when they depend on connecting with those of other people. In Research & Development nowadays, increasing effort is put into making it easy to 'go and see Fred or Mary' and to build on one another's work in the team.

Even physical positioning and layouts can operate as barriers, so research buildings are now being designed to make for open access and to increase the opportunities for informal chatting, where all 'rooms' open into a central space which everyone must always be crossing, making it highly likely to bump into one another. How the seating is arranged in a meeting may have profound consequences. Which way is 'up' and who sits where? How far away are they from one another: people can even be too close. What are the lines of sight? *For one famous United Nations meeting in Paris, weeks were spent just deciding on the shape of the table. The House of Commons is kept small, the left and right sides are arrayed against each other on purpose, to assure its adversarial character; and the power of the law is massively imposed by the design of the English courtroom.* The lecture hall is not one to encourage the people in serried ranks to initiate any new ideas—these have been rationed by the lecturer, though this is mitigated now by electronic messaging and voting.

Attention to such apparently material features is always amply repaid. Even when the size of the group is small and everyone is sitting behind tables in an open curve, the tables impose barriers that go farther than a physical constraint, and become an inhibitor. The German furniture company Metaplan of Quickborn made a business from this. They developed a whole genre of training furniture promoting idea-generation and discussion of thoughts posted up on the wall. By writing what mattered briefly, many could 'speak at once' and the freedom to walk around encouraged freedom of mind. I developed this concept further as *Visual Gathering*.

As the chairman of a major enterprise once complained to me, with twelve directors round the table and a meeting of ninety minutes' duration, anyone whose talking lasts more than seven minutes altogether is taking time from his colleagues. Everyone has to ration or stifle the thoughts they can share. This is why the apparently slow process of writing key thoughts instead of speaking them, and posting them up for all to see, can actually be more time-effective than talk alone.

Actually, most people who have to come with new thinking need to alternate between isolation in peace <u>and</u> coming together with others; individual people vary widely as to how much solitude or interaction they want, and for how long at a time. In any event, to get an idea conceived to be properly born into the world certainly needs support, development and implementation by many others, possibly over a long time-span.

"We need to work with partners who share our vision of meaningful innovation. That is why we actively pursue what we call Open Innovation—sharing our expertise and technical abilities with universities, institutes, and other companies so that, together, we can realize the very best ideas. We engage in two kinds of Open Innovation. Through 'inside-out' innovation, we make our skills and resources available to the outside world. Through 'outside-in' innovation, we draw on the capacities of individuals, organizations, and even small start-ups from around the globe." (A quote from the website of Philips.) What a change from the old policy of rigorous confidentiality that I followed for so many years of helping the company with invention and innovation.

4. Intellectual barriers

Then there is knowledge. The worst enemies of something new are not the managers and those who will use it with benefit, but the 'experts,' most of whom are at corporate center and act as middlemen at best and gatekeepers at worst. They are paid to know more, about less, than people in the fighting line, or 'coal-face,' and are responsible for preventing anything spoiling 'how things are done here.' Yet they are also charged with innovating in their specialist field—I have been one myself, as Manager Education & Training in Rank Xerox and then as Group Management Development Advisor, responsible for organization development for eighteen companies. I soon learned they must have both personal and organizational power, else much depends on whose initiative is at stake in the innovation.

As well as differing in temperament, people also vary in their style of thinking. This makes for huge clashes over any suggestion that is new. For the sake of simplicity, and without of course 'branding someone on their forehead' for life, we named anyone adopting the Reductive Relevance Box a *Reasoner*; the Stronger Box *Feelers*; and those trying to go beyond for unusual ideas, *Imagineers*. These labels represent their natural approach to a situation, which creates an intellectual barrier when it differs from yours, unless you are aware of this. This notion, especially the mutual opposition of logic and imagination, is explored in Chapters 3 and 14.

Devotees of the Reductive Box will not alter their frames of reference, nor let go of their disciplined thought enough to indulge in intuition. No, they need proof that abandoning their good processes could possibly be the way forward. Fantasy may be seen, by those who cannot distinguish between childish and child-like, as something only for children.

Properly so called, new 'information,' as well as being relevant or useful, must bring surprise. Yet this is clearly shocking to some people, who prefer a quiet life, one in which chaos is reduced to order, vagueness clarified, and you know where you stand. For such people anything 'new' or complex or ambiguous is confusing and inefficient. They control such thoughts by limiting the time they are willing to 'waste' on untried and untested data or notions. They might either judge an idea too soon or be too readily satisfied with the first idea that comes.

Customs and habits represent the line of least resistance, and the longer you live with them, the more you get grooved into the rut. The trouble is, some customs are genuinely effective, so not everyone is willing to resist the pressures of history and other people, to challenge what is popular or received wisdom.

5. New and old ideas are bound to conflict
Imagineers are striving for a new truth, one beyond what is known so far and accepted as right. This new truth is bound then to contradict received wisdom. This does not mean having to abandon reasoning altogether, but rather to do so for a moment, and only on purpose! If using logic has failed, you try an approach that puts judgment in suspense, knowing full well it will be the ultimate arbiter of whether something deserves to work or not. Anything that does work invariably turns out to be beautifully logical, but it requires 20-20 hindsight to find this out afterwards.

Years ago in Jutland, I presented a paper in a conference with the University of Aarhus with the provocative title of "What's Good about New?" Nothing necessarily so. What you already know can indeed help generate a new idea by unlearning what is apparently known, re-describing what you know, or re-positioning the perceiver. *If your old idea is that nothing moves faster than the speed of light, then you must rid yourself of this before claiming, for instance, that thought has a way of doing so.* (Of course it does!) Or else you must find some level, dimension or definition that can embrace two apparently opposing propositions. Actually, when you can do that, a new idea has been born. Indeed, when astrophysicists such as the Astronomer Royal Sir Martin Rees tell us about eleven dimensions, it seems sensible to ask, "Which are the extra seven?" (8 November 2008, Oxford Playhouse). And perhaps even to pursue whether, in recognizing new dimensions like string theory, another dimension has emerged—a twelfth?

To a scientist, Truth is constantly found to be a relative thing, a matter of probabilities, and time changes most notions. If we think of ideas as <u>not yet</u> significant, <u>no longer</u> realistic, possibly <u>not here</u> but there, then we can escape premature rejection. The history of science from Aristotle and Galen to the present day is full of changes in accepted truth. Even butter is now pronounced OK by all those nutrition and medical experts who tied it to obesity and forbade it!

6. Six dilemmas to resolve or modify one's attitude

1. Paradox over Probability.

To declare in your department that "If a job's worth doing, it's worth doing badly" you expect that you'll set the cat among the pigeons—especially with certain people. But wait! G K Chesterton was no fool. So what of all the things that never get done because of the <u>old</u> proverb? Surprise finds the edges and niches, identifying the subtle area where contrast begins and polarity ends. If you find the exceptional, it will put you ahead of the game. *Commute outwards, away from the city, buy shares that everyone is selling, seduce your enemy.* But take comfort in Murphy's other law: "Though a thing can go wrong, it might go better than you expected." Don't be caught out or taken aback by inability to cope with too much success. Why is 'abbreviation' such a long word?

2. Belief over Knowledge

We are trained to require facts, not opinion; they want quantitative proof, the evidence of experience. We expect completeness in reports, we believe with Occam in whatever requires fewer suppositions, and *No* is usually given more weight than *Yes*. Yet you only have to look at stock market behavior to see that 'behavioral economics' has overtaken stark rational analysis of fact, even in a supposedly rational arena.

3. Flexibility over Structure

Thinking, especially that of the Reasoner, has developed and been consolidated through structure. Structure is key to ensuring that things don't collapse, so is ignored at your peril. (See J E Gordon's delightful book entitled *Structures or Why Things Don't Fall Down.*) However, it is also true that structures have to be flexible so as to retain their integrity under extreme stress or change: bridges and skyscrapers are notorious examples of failure here, before the learning curve of our engineers steepened dramatically. The design of the human body was always more advanced than the rigid, robotic Dalek. Yet we should not forget that Man has got where he has by making patterns of his environment, finding laws and formulae, giving order and direction to the chaotic jungle out there. His pioneer settlement controls the rivers, makes the lines straight, organizes everything and strives for predictability, repeatability and reliability. The farmer needs rules and storage for peace of mind, so he tames everything that is wild. When thinking, we normally follow some procedures or rules, even without being aware of them.

Educated people who obey the disciplines of a profession find it hard to recognize when it's better to be more flexible, especially when normative approaches aren't working and so something new is needed. This may only be reached by organic sensing rather than the strength of rigidity. In fact we must break up old patterns and mental pathways, seek different reference points, change our focus and direction and above all retain our mobility. Einstein's 'thought-experiments' assumed certain ambivalence and ambiguity, some autonomy or independence of 'the rules,' and had to be without commitment. It's a kind of mental role-playing, pretending that something might work, without of course being sure. If you are sure, you must already possess the evidence, so then it's not new.

4. Risk over Safety

Dr. Gauss created his bell curve of normal distribution in 1809 and there are special implications for inventiveness. To allow your imagination full flight, you must lower the need to feel safe and embrace more risk than usual. Security and stability inhibit breaking out of their comfortable mold. The Imagineer specializes in escaping from the obvious and the traditional, so as to find the safety in risk. A recent *Financial Times* article about research on women investors found them guilty of "reckless caution." It may be some years before we know whether there is more risk in Brexit or in staying within the European Union...

Although life is constantly taking us by surprise, reason left to itself would seek only the information most likely to be verifiable, true, relevant and useful. Yet this earth-bound approach to exploration prevents people seeing beyond, beneath and between what is immediate and apparent.

Figure 8.3. The rhinoceros charge (Rozalind Clippingdale)

In fact, to take no risk at all might be the most dangerous attitude of all. *When the rhinoceros is charging you at 40 miles per hour, you had better move and if you dare not take two feet off the ground at once, you cannot even run, never mind leap for safety!* The timid in spirit, like the desperately cautious driver, can be dangerous indeed. As the old joke goes, "prediction is hazardous, especially about the future"; people may cling to the main trunk of the tree, not going out on a limb even though the finest fruit be there. They 'act responsibly,' sticking with symmetry and balance. Interesting that research, for instance by Donald McKinnon at Berkeley, has shown that creative people, compared with equally effective peers, had an in-built preference for the unstable, asymmetrical, unbalanced, disordered and chaotic. (See Barron/Welsh Art Scale.)

Of course, *even major tennis tournaments have been won by Wimbledon champions like Bjorn Borg and Chris Evert, who both returned everything with consistent groundstrokes from the baseline.* But most champions find the edges, placing their most powerful shots within millimeters of the line. When the chips are down, when there are no longer the resources you need, the palm goes to those who bear audacity and courage; especially when you are smaller than the opposition, what is both safer and most likely to succeed against the odds is surprise.

5. Conflict over Conformity

It is hard to argue against being realistic and sensible, disciplined and convergent on valid conclusions, with feet firmly on the ground. Caution is often sound, letting others make the running and all the mistakes. Many successful businesses, from IBM on, have been the wise follower. It is intelligent, not only emotional, to want majority approval, to be in fashion and to seek the protection of the herd, or the swarm. *Fishes keep swimming into the shoal to avoid being picked off at the outside by some predator; even lions go for the weakest laggards of the herd of wildebeest.* We not only conform to unconscious habit and instinct but also allow ourselves to be drawn towards some middle, even when asked to put various answers on a scale: psychometric tests and questionnaires need to be wary of a five or a seven point scale, because so many of us settle for three or four—it's called 'central tendency.' A scale of four or six points forces you off the fence, to come down one side or the other.

To reach the unusual, you stand apart from the herd, going against the stream. Even a chairman of a bank, a client of mine, memorably wrote in his Annual Report, "The status quo is not the way forward." In fact, being unorthodox, unconventional and unpredictable are hallmarks of those who are most forward-looking.

6. Jumping Ahead of Reason

Change that is evolutionary is usually more sound than the dramatic, revolutionary change. Yet the former might not ever reach its tipping point, while the latter has the force of excitement about it. Time compression can be a key factor: *compared with a smart blow from a hammer, steady pressure, unless huge, will fail to drive the nail into the timber; indeed, even an electric rotary drill is less effective than a hammer-drill.*

To reach some unknown idea, you may need to jump ahead of being reasonable, confident that someone will find why you are right, afterwards. Breakthroughs in battle are often made by first establishing a bridgehead, and only then firming up the supply lines. This is what justifies working on a hunch, and scientists and inventors have often worked like that. Boldness is king.

To sum up

Creativity finds the input which is too unusual, unlikely or obscure for it to be found by merely rational search. To ignore this paradox of reality means that our very skills and conventions of the intellect can present a major barrier to new ideas. Analysis and reason give control over and confidence in processing hard information into sound output: you can depend on it to catch all the obvious ideas, but not the surprising ones. *Be aware that criminals who evade being found out do not repeat their own habits, nor work along the lines of police protocol. Police success comes from thinking up how those clever criminals might do things differently.*

The higher the barriers, the greater the ingenuity in rising above them. Make sure you do not suffer from 'hardening of the categories'—the tighter they are, the narrower their contents, the more you have to reach outside the category. In Formula One racing, making the car or the circuit safer actually takes the gilt off the gingerbread, just as we are more amazed by the trapeze artist who has no net—though he might need the confidence it brings, to perform incredible feats.

Keep in mind: the tougher the test, the more confidence it gives you when you've passed it.

Chapter 9
Shock: The Certainty of Surprise

Surprise wins and without it, data simply does not inform. Exceptional results often stem from paradox, ingenuity and humour, all with the unexpected in common. Though it works through shock, wit brings fun and its motivation, and may even loosen a difficult inter-personal problem. It's a way to confront probability which so often stands in the way of a new truth, which is elusive mainly because of what we expect. If unintended consequences are so common, why not exploit them in advance, so as to take the problem by surprise?

1. Think otherwise or else!

Surprise is the only thing, apart from death and taxes, I can feel certain about. When my plan fails it is usually due to the impact of something unexpected. Of course it makes sense to avoid being taken by surprise—but it makes even more sense to take the problem by surprise! So rather than play off the back foot and suffer being the victim, why not get my retaliation in first? This way I keep the initiative and feel more on top of events. If I am up against impossible odds, without any chance or more resources, maybe I can win with questions that come from somewhere else, that seek something unusual.

"Art is serious play"

GRAYSON PERRY, POTTER, BBC REITH LECTURE 2013

We need to turn beyond 'critical thinking,' to seek the new paradigm of 'thinking otherwise.' Go for close contrast, or extreme cognitive violence: the most unlikely thought, like outrageous wit, can be the winner, and paradox is king. Needless to say, this also works in reverse: the problem can be a scorpion and catch you by surprise, so it can work as a subtle defense. "I am an Italian—but there's very little I can do about that!" (Renzo Piano, architect of The Shard, London, 2012).

Suppose you have to resolve intense competition between an immovable object and an irresistible force—you have a wicked problem. Normally I frown hard, grit the teeth, engage all limbs and organs, especially those that are of no help. Now I must violate the disciplines of my upbringing, job and profession, for only a distorting lens will show the insight I need. Exploit the fact that outcomes are so often the opposite of intention. The most famous medal in international ice-skating was won by Torvill and Dean with their astonishing performance set to Ravel's "Bolero" see Figure 9.1. Having honed their performance over many months of preparation, they had to cut Ravel's original music and even then it was just a little too long: skating time was officially limited to four minutes. Now, until skate touches ice, the stopwatch doesn't start, so they both began the performance on their knees! The triumph of it still resounds after so many years, and it was the first to be awarded top marks by every single judge. Phew! But it was not cheating—just unusual confrontation.

Figure 9.1. Torvill & Dean: Olympics gold

A kind of mental judo might alter the course of normal thought, making a full frontal assault with creative questioning, to include really subtle feints of mind. Such questions will have to be different from ordinary rational thinking, acting simply as stimuli, probes, and possible triggers for a domino of associations. Instead of one straight, narrow route to 'the truth,' there are always many possible ways to reach any one idea. Bletchley Park cracked the Enigma and Lorenz codes, thereby shortening World War II and leading to the first electronic computer. The rigorous detail and logic of those heroes working with Alan Turing was accelerated both by a few giant leaps and by many haphazard jumps. Creative questions, you can take 'em or leave 'em, using those that appeal and ignoring the rest. Such an approach is not allowed for logical questions.

Following Claude Shannon, 'Information' (that is, whatever informs a conclusion) entails some purpose that makes data meaningful through an element of surprise, which brings to awareness something new. Now, if a solution follows logically on from what is known, it will become obvious to anyone intelligent who focuses their attention on the problem. But diffi-culties never faced before, or where information is hidden or remote, need assault that catches them off-balance. Tactics to violate ordinary common sense are very common in war and other areas of competition and high achievement. To maximize the astonishment, you even build the expectation so as to dupe and mislead even more, increasing the success of the trickery. We see this not only in fencing with rapiers, but also in rugby, all racquet games—and of course in chess, a war game! The more normal and rational the approach of your friend or adversary, the easier it is to lead him astray and take him aback. There's usually some hidden information or a little extra twist to secure the *coup de grace*, but always you seize the problem by the throat and resolve it in some unusual way.

In the quest for originality, motivation and energy are vital, especially because you need courage to stick with an original idea in the face of the conservative majority. Throwing away one's own old ideas often means you are throwing away ideas also held by other people, whom you will need, to win acceptance and forward momentum. "If we want things to stay as they are, things will have to change" (Giuseppe di Lampedusa, 1896–1957). One evening I asked my wife what was for dinner. "Something different, as usual" was her reply—she is amazingly versatile with her menus: one day she might say, "Same as last Tuesday, for a change!"

2. Wit and humor

There is a long and rich tradition, in England particularly, of the natural and effortless flow of wit; close study of what is entailed reveals remarkable similarities with the genius for inventiveness that has also been a tradition here. It is amazing how many breakthroughs in science and technical products have sprung out of this small island off the coast of Europe, ever since the founding of the Royal Society in the 17th century and the Industrial Revolution in the 18th. Such a pity the UK goes to the bottom of the class when it comes to buy-in of our own inventions—America is tops for that.

There is this strange connection between imagination, surprise and humor. A detective story would be spoiled if you revealed in advance that the actual murderer was the butler. When it is the president who slips on the banana skin, it is funny only because his dignity makes it incongruous. For the medieval king, one person with special power was the fool, the only man in court who got away with whatever he said because he thought round corners, with unexpected twists and turns, so was highly valued by the king. Why not play the jester to get your own back on Chance? That's the fun, and the utility.

Figure 9.2. The Jester (Cecil William Rhodes)

"Behind every great man is a surprised woman." (Maryon Pearson) Wit has been defined as "using unexpected associations between contrasting or disparate words or ideas, to make a clever humorous effect." Perhaps this is why so many ingenious, inventive people are full of wit, unconventional, contrarian and only tolerable when their suggestions are not just wild but shrewd, when they are such fun and yet actually work. An older meaning of this Anglo-Saxon word is about seeing, what we call insight. Moreover, wit entails much more than jokes: it holds the mystic sense of practical, ingenious wisdom, being shrewd and clever—"He didn't have the wit to…" We speak of 'his rapier wit' because his mind flashes fast in and out before you can gasp. It comes from a strange or even opposite direction, to take a short cut. "The impossible just takes a little longer" (George Santayana) or is defeated faster than you expect.

When you actually say something as it is, it's so often funny, for wit includes saying it straight when that is not expected; *I well remember at Oxford how Brian Boobbyer, the English rugby player, so often outwitted the defense by going straight forward instead of across the field as was normal.* Two favorite broadcasters of mine are Garrison Keillor, of Lake Wobegon fame and Clive James, the wry Australian writer. Wit is epitomized by radio comedy programs live on BBC, such as "I'm Sorry I Haven't a Clue" chaired for decades by the famous jazz band leader, Humphrey Lyttelton; as a contrast to these impromptu performances was the brilliant script-writing team of Frank Muir and Denis Norden.

Creativity has many features in common with jokes, including having a serious purpose and operating on many levels:
1. Conceiving a brilliant idea is like thinking up the joke
2. Developing it so that it works is like ensuring there are no weak elements or loose ends and the punchline is timed well
3. Making it accepted by colleagues is like getting them to actually laugh
4. Recognizing a promising idea when you meet one is like 'getting it'
5. Spinning off further applications beyond the original idea is like developing its variations. (An analysis of jokes has revealed that all of them derive from just six originals!)

When telling a joke, you purposely do not explain the relevance of certain small but crucial splinters in your story, which only come home with the punch line. Nor do you explain it afterwards to anyone who failed to 'see the joke.' Surprise is the thing, and you risk much to achieve it, as when Gerald Ratner lost a fortune from his jewelers retail business with his joke about a decanter he called a "crap product."

The most serious issues are sometimes best resolved with humor, and on the instant too. In spite of our 'work ethic,' people actually do their best work when they feel it's like play. When work is merely dutiful and worthy, it is likely to be dull, for excitement is important, with color, sparkle and praise. One can even define work as activity where the motivation comes from outside the person, something that <u>has</u> to be done; play is what you do for fun—but those people who <u>find</u> the play in their work sustain what really matters to them and achieve outstanding results. Why should I retire, when I'm enjoying my work so much?

The epitome of ingenuity is to be flagrantly unorthodox, even if this disconcerts other people as much as does the problem. The arts of deception, of camouflage, of illusion and allusion might well be used inside out, to uncover ideas that would otherwise elude our search. The risk is worth taking, not only to escape pedestrian thoughts but to seize the astonishing. We do this fully aware and with permission, for feeling and emotion are of huge importance to imagination.

How on earth to illustrate a chameleon against its background?!

The shock tactics being discussed here can be anathema to people's values, because it seems to work by cheating, to be undeserved, by exploring an unseen horizon or even thinking inside out, against the stream or backwards. No wonder the person being creative can be the despair of their normal, rational colleague. Of course the others don't always see the joke, so reject the idea. No wonder the initial idea can fail at one time, in a certain environment, yet become a breakthrough in other circumstances.

So the would-be inventor uses variations of this 'wit' to strive for some blinding incongruity. This might be the only way to discover what is new or not-true-yet, to realize an unrecognized truth, to bring it into mind and make it real. Images of all kinds show us implications beyond what can be observed. *In crossword puzzles, clues are ingeniously designed to provide 'almost-information,' needing the player to ask what is significant about what is <u>missing</u>*. Yes, to be creative involves playing a kind of game, only that, when fully engaged, it feels more than a matter of life or death. The mix is alchemy, but it works.

3. The value of paradox

"India brought nothing into the world."

The speaker meant, of course, the concept of zero. By making mischief among the whole armory of intellectual processes, we seek the double-edged paradox that alone may solve the problem we face. Here are some examples.

- The old Latin tag *Festina lente*, or 'Make haste slowly,' has a great deal more wisdom than is shown by the impetuous young novice.
- The makers of (genuine) Hoover carpet-cleaning machines advised their too-energetic users that "The slower you move it, the faster it cleans" and this is still true
- All men in prison have hours of freedom every day, to do things for which the rest of us are too busy

- Shakespeare warns that "The lady doth protest too much, methinks"
- The self-righting lifeboat was feared by its crews because of what it did to the men inside her
- Building drainage systems lowers the water table, whilst removing bottlenecks in major roads simply invites more traffic
- The best way to hit something is sometimes to aim away from it
- The arrow will carry farther from a bow of metal than of flexible yew
- The ball of steel will bounce higher than one of rubber
- The most likely food to lose a tooth in will not be anything hard, but something soft, like a bread roll!

Ever since William of Occam, the 13/14th century friar, we have preferred to go with whatever proposition puts the least strain on our credulity. Reason has a tendency to prefer the clean, obvious relationship between cause and effect and anything else is suspect. It is the iron grip of probability that one needs to escape from in order to increase the chances of coming up with an original thought, other than serendipity. We need to invite the chance of stumbling onto unexpected findings, like the moment when a researcher utters what the science fiction writer Isaac Asimov called, "the most exciting phrase in science": *That's funny!* Of course he didn't mean humorous, but peculiar or strange. Recall that the word 'sinister' used to mean just 'on the left' but because left-handedness is strange, the meaning became 'evil' or 'treacherous.' Our normal upbringing with so-called 'critical thinking' skills has placed a premium on probability. How likely is something to be true or to deliver what we intend, and how provable is it? Scientific training demands a certain kind of a limited form of evidence from observable experience.

Here are some more illustrations:

- Driving accidents are more likely to occur on black ice than in snow, on parts of the road that <u>seem</u> safe, rather than on steep bends; slight camber variations are more dangerous than a really bad road.
- For a long time, motorcars were built with strong bumpers or fenders to protect very directly against collision. Now they are designed to maximize the damage to the car caused by the slightest little bump to keep the repair shops in business. No, not really! They are now

supposed to crumple progressively so as to absorb the impact and protect the people within.

- Boats naturally try to keep all the water out and avoid being swamped: the raft lets all the water through and so cannot be sunk. Thus the racing dinghy can sail herself out of being swamped by letting the inboard water out through holes in the stern.
- The fencer feints in one direction and thrusts in another; and in certain martial arts, the greater the force of your opponent, the worse he suffers from your deft agility.
- To be safe from the enemy, it's more usual to keep your distance. When Drake's small force inflicted so much damage on the huge fleet of Spanish Men O' War in Cadiz, he did so in spite of all the guns around the harbor, by sailing in so close that his ships could not be fired upon.
- In World War II, Singapore's powerful seaward defenses were made irrelevant when the Japanese army took it from behind.
- It is a paradox that the least likely brings the most success. This may bring to mind Pareto's 80/20 law, that, for instance, you get 80% of your business from 20% of your customers. When Pareto brought this mathematical formula to notice, it was a revelation, and whilst it cannot work on everything, it certainly makes one look harder for the insight in each situation which may overturn what we expect, or outwit the situation.

The trick is to spot the niche that converts disaster into triumph. And it usually is a narrow edge, demanding an exciting flash of conceptual aggression, which most people are loath to risk. In music, the intentional discord or dissonance produces a delicious frisson of pleasure which is often more effective than a straightforward harmony. In like manner, the clash of opposites brought by the oxymoron carries far more clout than a phrase flowing smoothly. "Another victory like that and we're done for" ejaculated Pyrrhus, as he surveyed all his casualties strewn around. Tough love, the cruelty of kindness, so-called 'emotional intelligence,' all follow in a long tradition. If only it were accurate that the Chinese character depicting 'crisis' also expressed 'opportunity' (John F Kennedy).

4. My crisis is your opportunity?

Exponents of unconventionality are called eccentrics or oddballs. Jazz players are seen as angular, quirky, unconventional, far out, and of course witty. When behavior is so incongruous as to be 'in your face,' we speak of gall. As in judo, a basic ploy is to use the strength of opposing forces to <u>help</u> us surmount them or spring beyond them. Referring to the global financial crisis of 2007–9, the *Financial Times* urges us "To avoid mistakes, take the advice of those who made them!" Use the very force of the wind against you to sail faster still than you could if it were blowing you forward. Yes, you can! I have tried out this phenomenon with many hundreds of able managers, most of whom react to such a suggestion as if it couldn't possibly work—but that's the point, especially when you hope to reach an idea that others wouldn't. Sailing downwind, a yacht's speed is slightly slower than wind-speed because of hull drag, and there is no chance of actually going faster than what is driving you. But pointing somewhat <u>against</u> the wind uses vector mathematics, so that the boat prefers to move forward rather than against the drag force of the keel. Then the sail also acts like an airfoil or the wing of a plane. And finally the wind-speed adds to the boat-speed, rather as when two cars crash from opposite directions, the impact is much greater than the speed of either. Sailors know there is more to it than this, but I hope to make the simple point: you don't need such a high wind-speed to reach over 65 knots.

Figure 9.3. sailing on the wind

Less is more. There are thousands of variations on this well-known theme so this is a skill one has to learn. It took a long while to discover that most storage systems prove to be a way to store air at great expense, so we now have 'ready-to-assemble' furniture. Animals at the head of the food chain, like the tiger, are those needing protection, else they will become extinct, whilst insects are more numerous than any other living creatures. Yet on the other side, redundancy in engineering is sometimes vital, especially from the point of view of the astronaut on his way to the stars! One was heard to remark wryly that every single piece of equipment in his space ship had been purchased at the lowest tender price…

Think of all those things, from steam and electricity Before Christ to the laser of yesterday, which did not seem to have a market at the time. And before you ejaculate that steam is past it, be aware that it is today the essential ingredient in thousands of manufacturing operations around the world. The Spirax Sarco range is enormous, including combined heat and power, oil refining and processing, industrial and agri-chemicals, pharmaceuticals, hospitals, food, brewing, distilling and dairy, cars and aircraft, electronics, textiles, paper, rubber and plastics, ceramics and glass, print, paints and packaging, tobacco and sugar, water treatment. Goodness! Today in the 21st century, due to its high heat-carrying capacity, controllability, sterility and efficiency for heat transfer, steam is the natural choice in most industries. Isn't that surprising? Paper documents are proliferating in the age of the computer—just as I remember the consumption of carbon paper actually went up when Xerox brought photocopying to the world.

Akin to the concept of remote connection, introduced in Chapter 13, is to find the most unlikely ways to succeed, and you escape the probabilities, not by running away but by confronting them. This creates extreme tension in violating current knowledge and judgment by finding a chink; only it does so with such cunning force as to bring out of the extrusion unexpected but outstanding results. Often you feel a delicious elegance, as "I managed to do it just outside the nick of time" (Susie Boyt, *Financial Times*).

A rich vein of humor has to run through science. "What scientists do is by its nature frustrating. They are trying to understand things that no one else has managed to understand. Much of the time they will fail at this, so it helps to have a sense of humour about yourself. When a scientist makes a really good, unexpected discovery, everyone else's first reaction is going to be laughter" (Mac Abrahams, founder in 1991 of the Ig Nobel Prize). What a title!

5. Irony

Here are three ways to read what Pasteur said:
"The trouble with <u>imagination</u> is that it is sometimes right"
    so What about judgment?
"The trouble with imagination is that it is sometimes <u>right</u>"
    so How do you know when it is wrong?
"The trouble with imagination is that it is <u>sometimes</u> right"
    so If only sometimes, should we really risk it? Or can we afford not to?

Both Economics and Psychology make the mistake of striving too hard to use mathematics to establish their academic respectability. "Take the math out of economics and you get closer to real life." This seems incongruous, but such irony is used to make a telling point. It's done with our eyes wide open, evoking enough shock to exploit the thin vein of precious metal in hard rock. This strategy reveals the unexpected and is certainly worth its weight in gold. Wisdom is often uttered with irony. "It is dangerous to be right on matters in which the established authorities are wrong" (Voltaire The age of Louis XIV).

> *"Language was given us so as to conceal our thoughts."*
> CHARLES TALLEYRAND

Ironic humor is a form of internal dissonance, having the force of the discord in music. "The weather remains changeable" (BBC forecast). Alan Bennett declared that "gossip is the acceptable face of intellect"—he is an Englishman! Of course, we all have our own tactics, and not everyone loves irony. Perhaps Winston Churchill's wit was more appreciated on his side of the Atlantic than the other when he famously said, "The United States always does the right thing—after having exhausted all other possibilities." At least his own mother was American… Yet irony can be a shrewd ally. Who can resist Lord Chesterfield when in the 18th century he was heard saying, "We, my Lords, may thank God that we have something better than our brains to help us run the country." More than two centuries later, when a politician uses the word 'fairness' to claim the moral high ground, we are still working through the full implications of George Orwell's 1984 slogan, "All animals are equal, but some animals are more equal than others." The Senate of Rome declared that justice carried to extremes becomes injustice. I love the thought that one should not carry even moderation to extremes.

6. Deception

Deceiving other people is rightly seen normally as a bad thing, but reaching a new idea entails finding something different, so there's nothing wrong in borrowing from the arts of illusion and deception, in a good cause. Remember that when you are only wondering, no judgment is being used, so it is impossible to be wrong. How disarming! After all, our first perceptions often turn out to be illusions, so it is worth seizing the opportunity to become right unusually, even unusually right. The great Repton held, "Deception is key to landscaping, gardening and architecture." As Machiavelli advised, what's good about deception is that it so often works. The conjuror relies on subverting your perceptions. Lies are told or tricks performed by making appearances deceptive.

Figure 9.4. The wily serpent

Some more examples:

- Just as camouflage prevents being noticed and perhaps hit by enemy gunfire, so politicos are ever resorting to smoke and mirrors.
- Changing the label for something contentious is often done when politicians resort to 'spin.' They employ euphemisms like 'asylum seekers' as word-images to blur the truth about immigration that may be either illegal or sought only for economic reasons, so that protesters can be branded as racist and thus defeated in a decent society.
- Frequently, ingenuity is mobilized in the form of political correctness to influence how the public thinks: George Orwell in *Nineteen Eighty-Four* was so prophetic.
- The UK government's handling of the issue of joining the euro was treated almost entirely as a fiscal or currency decision, so that the real, political issue was kept in the background. It is very plausible, since after all the euro is a currency.
- There was said to be no reliable evidence that the North Sea is polluted—though the River Maas was so heavily nourished from the chemical factories upstream in Switzerland and Germany that a Dutchman famously developed a film in its waters!
- The validity of Gulf War Syndrome was long denied.

Over-zealous use of would-be 'scientific' testing can actually work against establishing the truth. This can be worse than over-zealous imagination, because it involves Judgment and therefore Action. Another way to hide the truth is to conceal it in a welter of needless 'information' so that the tree cannot be noticed for the wood around it. Are the acres of small print for any financial transaction for the benefit of customers, or made with fell intent, under the cloak of the Financial Conduct Authority? You can also slip in an adjective that the public might miss—as when Arthur Scargill, the mineworkers' leader, claimed that the UK had the cheapest <u>deep-mined</u> coal in the world. This was actually true—but nobody noticed the adjective <u>deep-mined</u> so were successfully misled, for year after year. Whatever, we can harness the tactics of deception, to reach new perspectives and ideas, including wrong ones...

7. Unintended consequences

We speak of the 'law of unintended consequences' when the outcome of a carefully planned initiative is quite different from what we had been aiming at. This is astonishingly common in national interventions in the economy.

- In the UK it is sad that indefinite support for those not working has led to massive swelling of an underclass, as unfair on them as on the rest of the community supporting them.
- Equally well-meaning governments attempted to make it easier for everyone to own their own home by making significant tax concessions for mortgages: even the less well off should benefit. Result: steep and continuing rise in the prices people were willing to pay for housing, and the costs are now so high as to put a home of their own out of reach for many people, especially in London.
- I remember a cartoon where the biology master is glaring at the frog sitting at the desk in front of him. "Good heavens, Brown, how many times have I told you to find the antidote before starting an experiment?" It would indeed be wise. This principle should be embodied in every law, and every regulation should be future-proofed to avoid its dire consequences.
- In medicine, we have carried out so much preventive injection that people's immune systems might now be at risk. Antibiotics are in danger of being overcome by clever bugs that we have been training up.
- Schools and parents that abandoned discipline so as not to curb creativity have made the children's natural ingenuity almost vestigial.
- Detergent used to combat oil slicks from tankers (or drilling for oil) at sea has proved more harmful in many cases than the oil it dispersed. Thankfully, these slicks are very visible, so they have accelerated ecological defense measures, turning a disaster to good account after all.

Like the contrarian investor who seeks the opportunity to buy shares when they are going down and everyone is selling them, the Imagineer turns the skills of the Reasoner to good account by spotting the flaw in the trend, finding some exceptions to the pattern, discerning something unusual about a company, which overturns or reverses predictions and turns them inside out. Fire can be produced by using a block of ice as a lens. Selective weed killer on lawns encourages excessive <u>growth</u> of the weeds, which thus exhausts them and they die. Like an acrobat or a Houdini escapologist, the Imagineer uses the very weight of evidence-based reason against itself so as to carry off the astonishing feat. The magician wins through intense attention to detail. We must discover what nuclear waste is <u>good for</u>, making it sought after or safe and profitable.

In certain cases, logic might work in reverse, and this offers hidden opportunities.

- Victor Parnes tells the anecdote of a man whose neighbor kept him awake until 2 in the morning with loud music. He did not fret and fume or bang on the wall or shout at his neighbor to stop. Instead, he phoned him at 5 a.m. to say how much he had enjoyed the music.
- Following Marks & Spencer's penny stall and Woolworths' 'nothing over sixpence' the Walmarts of today are rife with loss-leaders.
- 'Ethical businesses' such as the Triodos Bank can even attract more money than they can find opportunities to invest.
- Maybe you do become rich by giving away all you have, even if this was not Christ's intention. By the way, I noticed this imperative in church recently: *Give to God what's right, not what's left.*"

Question: "How many Oxford dons does it take to change a light-bulb?"
Answer: "Change? Change! Who said anything about change?"
(Only graduates of Oxford are allowed such jokes—but it's a universal.)

Chapter 10

Just Change

To change what you already have or know is far easier than to create an idea out of nothing. Dig out all those assumptions, the deadweight of baggage that keeps so many ideas out of bounds, and challenge them with specific questions. Think up how many ways you could describe what you 'know' and then, if you cannot find the edges and exceptions, exploit all the permutations possible. Then question what you previously held to be 'good' about it, whether you are treating it as fact or belief, and whether your issue is easy or difficult. You already have thousands of options.

How can one reach new ideas on demand? Can anyone really create out of nothing? Any new idea can feel very elusive and ephemeral, but you can take something that already exists and change it. Multi-choice questions are far easier to answer than open questions that require you to think something up! They use them in exams, not only to make marking easier than for essays, but also, we suspect, to dumb it down and get more children higher grades!

In practice, it is always easier to see what to change from than think up what to change to. Rather than attempt to whistle something up out of thin air, everyone can produce exceptional results by taking an unusual look at whatever they have experienced. New concepts come by the force of extrusion and by manipulating your normal thoughts in direction, space, time, extent and force. When the challenge of your situation is high, then ingenuity is your trump card: in fact fewer resources demand resourcefulness. An engineer belongs to a noble profession, one that begets things, by contriving: in France, he is an *Ingenieur*, the ingenious one—if not a man of genius?

An important faculty here is energy for change. We make gaps that weren't there and bridge others with great mental leaps. Imagineers more likely feel that if it could be, then it should, and they believe in the surplus energy or spark which will jump the gap to the idea. Obviously if nobody knows what should happen nor notices what actually has, there is no energy for a new solution. This is a sign that people, organizations or countries are in decline.

1. In which mood?
You call on imagination when you need to doubt natural perceptions because they do not favor you—or in case they might! "*When we can't out-spend our competitors, we can out-think them.*" Ideas cannot be creative in themselves, for what is brilliant or elusive for one person is obvious to another, or at another time or place. So it is more practical to see creativeness in the approach of the person concerned. Because most of us are barely conscious of how we are thinking at any moment, any unusual ideas we have often suffer from our failure to realize how 'creative' they might be. Therefore we do not take enough trouble to build that bridge from the strange to the familiar that people need before they will recognize the value of anything original, that is, outside their norms.

It's important to gain conditions under which newly born notions can survive long enough to be judged properly as to whether they would be worth developing and adopting. This applies not only when trying to generate ideas with other people, but also even on your own, especially if you have high standards. It is astonishing how the remains of pride and duty and feeling responsible conspire against even jotting down an idea that might seem worthless in one context. To say that you are brainstorming is not enough—people have to learn and experience just what it means and feels like to brainstorm well.

Even to consider a radically different approach, most of us need an open declaration to escape from the disciplines of our upbringing, our job and profession. Independent of judgments made in the past, I am planting a rebel flag. This is divergent thought, the mirror image of convergent: opening up to possibilities you might otherwise discount as impossible, not testing a conclusion before acting on it. You might have to re-position yourself or unlearn what is apparently known.

New ideas are dangerous, so to voice one we need a safety net, as when walking a tightrope, that will enable us to be more daring and versatile. This confidence comes from the knowledge that any idea you reach will be subject to the rigorous scrutiny of description and judgment. *Rest a six-inch wide board on two chairs and it's so easy to walk the plank: place the same plank 100 feet up on scaffolding and then try it. It is exactly as easy to do—except for the consequences!* When you go into special mode, there are no consequences. So leaving the reasonable self with feet realistically in the mud, we leap ahead of reason, shooting a silken thread of an idea to the top of the cliffs, whence we hope to haul up the practical rope attached to it. Such a metaphor may encourage us to recognize that we often need something quite wild and insubstantial at first, the silken thread, to lead onto a stronger idea, the rope, that might bear some weight. The arrow could not first have carried the heavier rope so high and far. But later you might use its strength, to bring on something more sound. "I am often wrong, but why not try this…?"

2. Challenge assumptions
Most of us carry a lot of baggage, preventing us from being original, so it needs a positive kick before we can get 'normal practice' and experience out

of our mind. We don't want what we had and knew to be an undue burden, restraining any effort to acquire something new. So this weight must be thrown overboard, jettisoned or at least challenged. We hope to change our accepted wisdom, to discover unusual connections and relationships in the universe outside, and to go farther and deeper than ever before. But to exploit them fully we must first release ourselves from prisons of the past. Trouble is, you cannot fight what you cannot see, so we have to uncover assumptions we are not aware of, and that needs skill.

While it is essential to put on this mood of rebellion and actively ignore ancient custom, it often helps also to mount a more concrete and positive attack on old shibboleths. Well, here's the rub: strongly held constructs and convictions are assumptions buried deep within ourselves. They throw differing lights upon our impressions that will bias, steer and limit our experiencing. But if we can dig them out, we can challenge whether each one still applies to the particular issue at hand, for if not, it offers an open field for potential solutions so released.

"Say No to No" (Shell advertisement). The accepted wisdom of experience, or the industry, or of science and other sacred cows, has to be confronted by adopting the role of a heretic or maverick. Cut the knots, strike the shackles, question the rules. But still test in case the rule be valid, and if not you can then let rip. Is the way it has always been done the best? Do we really have to obey this rule? How certain are you that the future will turn out like that?

Trends and herds are forms of assumption, with its dangers of non-thinking. As fashion and mass marketing show, the herd instinct is still going strong: *starting out as a gesture, jeans quickly became for practical purposes a 'uniform' for the young, just as the current fashion of wearing a suit tie-less is now de rigueur if you want to appear approachable.* Even the 'flavor of the month' has to be followed, as if we were sheep or lemmings. We keep looking sideways at our neighbors, lest we are out in front or stand out from the crowd. Indeed it seems that when the Millennium Bridge opened across the Thames, the throngs of people crossing it tended to fall into step, so that the bridge began to sway from left to right, taking on the alarming rhythm known as 'resonance,' which is a kind of technical 'empathy'; so additional stabilizers had to be installed. In discussions between two people, their gestures and behavior often begin to copy or mirror each other. We must conform, and we go with the majority, not just for democratic reasons, but also for safety and social acceptability. Standing alone against the stream, challenging orthodox views or fashions is akin to 'sending yourself to Coventry.'

It is really hard to suspend judgment. Attempting to not-use judgment often fails: as when someone says to you *"Do not even think of a pink elephant."*

- To learn a new habit, we must withhold the old one—yet just try to not-write your own signature well enough to deceive a forensic scrutiny. As Arthur Koestler said, "The human nervous system is a habit-forming machine."
- If you ever move to a house near the railway, after a while you have no trouble in sleeping. But the first night the 3.30 a.m. milk train is discontinued, you leap out of your deep sleep, crying, "What was that?!"
- And there is the taxi-driver who on his way to a certain address arrived at the street to find it marked One Way against him. Only when he had completed his detour did he realize he was actually on foot…

A habit is a rut which you have to get out of to avoid doing the same old thing. Old ideas and images hold you back and prevent you from allowing strange ideas to enter your head, so you must deal with them to win your freedom.

Consider the layout of your computer keyboard. It is probably QWERTY, the same as the English language typewriters for the past century. They have always been like that. But do they really have to be? Is this layout a valid imperative? Certainly not—in fact it was designed so as to slow down the good typist whose fingers were faster than the keys could go without jamming. Most assumptions were originally reasonable, but questioning their validity for <u>this concern</u> opens up an opportunity. So with hydroponics we can actually grow food in rocky desert land, because plants don't always need soil.

Challenging your own assumptions is difficult because you cannot fight what you cannot see, so you can steal the analytic tools of the Reasoner to fire the questions at yourself. But it's easier to harness friends and colleagues to question you, and persist until you answer them. They do not even have to know the details of your problem to raise questions such as:

- What unconscious beliefs from the past might stop you exploring certain ideas?
- Have you done anything like this before?
- Has it always been done this way—surely there could be exceptions?
- Can I smell a sacred cow here and what if you ignore it?
- Where is the absolute standard that has to be obeyed?
- What facts have you accepted that concern the future?
- Will ignoring any of your assumptions bring certain failure of the solution?

Effective Intelligence, the product of my research, offers a whole suite of such questions, all of which can be used without knowing a thing. They lead into the sources for those hidden assumptions—why you would otherwise be blind to the opportunities they are concealing. The more 'expert' the owner of the problem is, the more assumptions have been chaining their minds and so the more new options will be revealed. Of course, only the owner of the problem can say whether any assumption found is genuine here or not. And this approach appeals to Reasoners themselves, because you have borrowed their clothes to test their version of reality and revealed their lacunae.

Other sources of unconscious assumptions include the rules you must work within, how you interpret causal relations, and your predictions for the future. As I write, the issue in the UK whether or not to exit from the European Union is full of guesses and predictions as to how it would affect our economy—all treated as facts, but falsely so, because they cannot have happened yet.

3. Exceptions

All generalizations harbor exceptions (!) We never say never, or everywhere or all the time, and especially not 'all.' There are kinds of something, parts of anything, phases of any action plan. Many new ideas come from extremes of accuracy and precision, the persistent scrutiny of some detail that turns out to make all the difference. The evolution of skis offers more than one example of this phenomenon of creativity. Years ago I assumed that skis would go faster the smoother they could be made: surely friction slows them down, for I remember owners of the old Thames barges actually using black lead on the hull when preparing for the famous North Sea races. It seemed a reasonable assumption. But this was challenged, first by introducing a subtle ripple effect and more recently by widening the leading edge of the ski. Both inventions successively gave significant competitive advantage to their skiers.

So always check which chamber of your revolver is not loaded, before firing. We often fail to ask where something is OK, precisely when would something become unsafe, how much of a drug is not to be recommended. One reason is of course we are unable to identify well enough the boundary between what is true and what you might expect, but it ain't the case. Even harder is to think up what one should expect, for it is valid.

There is more to this point. All designers, in considering how their new product should work better than any other, expect to take account of several parameters of space and time and extent, what they hope to make and what it's for. Yet even if they spend months and years on the details, only the best explore for each of these parameters enough about exceptions, including what they do <u>not</u> want. This is often what sorts the men from the boys, revealing the shaft of brilliant insight that eluded those not willing to use more imagination. How often do you yourself try to think of the <u>worst</u> way of doing something? And what does that tell you?

Figure 10.1. New from old

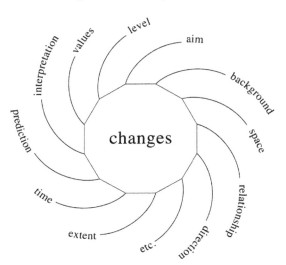

4. Change your description

For some, attacking convention is the fun, and they assume that something unique will be better. You break out of existing patterns, or the tramlines that make you think in only two possible directions; you change the direction of your mental gaze, describe from a different viewpoint. Then you will see it in a different light, from a different angle, for a different function, and so on. Your (metaphorical) field of vision needs changing, and you can do this sort of thing on purpose, on demand.

Even a computer may be programmed to generate other options by changing patterns of description, so Man had better keep ahead of the game! All our images have formed themselves into some kind of pattern in our mind. *Clouds are castles in the sky*. Exceptional effectiveness needs some kind of unusual analysis to penetrate beneath and beyond the facts and beliefs normally considered relevant. Ideas are born from changing the connections formed by experience. By making mischief among the whole armory of intellectual processes, we seek the double-edged paradox that alone can solve the problem we face.

In the years before he died, I was corresponding with Alex Osborn, author of *Applied Imagination* and founder of the Creative Education Foundation. He first made a following for brainstorming. A tool he thought up was to change your focus, your means and ends and your patterns with triggers such as magnify, minify and reverse; other uses and adapt; modify, re-arrange, substitute and combine. This might seem simple, but of course each trigger has several versions: re-arrange includes interchange components, layout, reverse, pace, time, cause-effect, head to tail, change the angle, etc. Checklists are a practical trick if you cannot get started or you run dry.

Basic grammar offers a further opportunity: change subject to object and you get "Man bites dog!"—a great headline. Change an adjective or adverb and the account of your event is fundamentally altered—listen harder to politicians! Prepositions like to and from, inside and outside, by and for... the list is very fruitful. Consider the difference between how much and how many—sometimes even reciprocal. And what of the most obvious construct of number? Just by changing the order of numerals, you can transform 14739 into 97134... Anyone can write new music simply by changing the notes, their timing, their loudness, which ones are played at once, and so on. And the alphabet makes possible a million words.

5. Morphology

Could a monkey with a typewriter really write Shakespeare? Permutation is a way to <u>use</u> imagination even if you don't have much of it. We are good at representing what we can already touch and see. A huge and complex variety of 'dimensions' has been built up or identified through science and the arts over the centuries with which we can identify, recognize, measure and replicate things. Even to focus only on the basic elements of What and Who, Where and When, How and How Much, with all their variations, anyone can change a description.

Morphology is the name given to a process used by Frank Whittle in developing the jet engine in the England of the 1920s. It is an almost 'mechanical' way to rearrange the ideas we hold into new patterns, of which the number is infinite. *Just to permutate the football results of the English leagues was complex enough to create a kind of gambling lottery, the 'pools.'* Color only one side of a diagonal across a tile, and it will offer hundreds of patterns. So this technique generates options by combining elements and parameters that are key to the invention. Suppose you wanted to design a new kind of screen for your computer, to enable a large audience to view it, instead of a few huddling around. The factors to consider would represent what the screen must have or be or deliver; for instance support system, stiffness of material, shape, ease of assembly, portability, and suchlike. Then there could be several versions of each factor; for instance there are kinds of material that might be used, several ways to assemble and stow it, more than one possible shape, and so on. By making a matrix of these parameters and all their versions, you lay out all the possible permutations. Mathematically speaking, seven versions of seven parameters could yield as many as 250,000 possibilities. Like re-sorting variegated pebbles into different pockets, or spreading them out in diverse groupings, we find abstractions that match experience with some new idea. Such morphology has limits only of time. The secret is a tolerance of ambiguity, of not having to be absolute, complete or right. And who knows? You might go on beyond the roll-up screen for your computer and on to a smart phone that projects.

Figure 10.2. tile permutations

A genius is someone who puts known facts together in some unusual way. The point is, you can use this trick on anything that's worth some systematic generation of ideas. Leaving aside the jet engine, it's not really rocket science!

6. Inside out

Which was more important when you bought your house—what was inside or how it looked from outside? Was it your view or where it stood in its environment, what people outside see? The question 'What would be good for this goal?' if turned inside out becomes 'What would this be good for?' We name things by what they are useful for, so a tool for driving in screws is called a screwdriver. But is that all it can do? You could use it as a chisel or stab someone to death! Likewise, *we grasp the value of a motorcar tire, cut perfectly to grip the road and throw off water: this is what it was made for, though you can see it as part of the wheel, or of the suspension, and even the steering system.* But if we look harder at what tires are made of, their structure or how the constituent parts work together, and their other characteristics, such as weight and strength and hollowness, we quickly find a thousand other uses for them. Dumping them in a mound under the sea can afford shelter for fishes and crustaceans as well as a reef; they make perfect fenders, for boats and for the garage at home—your wife's, of course! Hanging them round a man's neck to set him alight was a terrifying punishment for people with 'wicked' political beliefs in South Africa.

Further, you can change those rules (Looking In) or change the game itself (Looking Out)—this is what happened at Rugby School, when a boy (wrongly) picked up the ball in a game of football. To escape a closed paradigm means to treat it as part of a larger or wider system, and it is that higher system that has to be obeyed. *Things that go up must come down, because of gravity.* Yet this rule can be apparently escaped by flying to a space station, where you may have to pull a tool down to use it. (Gravitational pull has not disappeared, but you have eluded the earth's system.) Could there be micro-systems too? Yes, subatomic physics offers many ways in which normal Newtonian rules are reversed or do not apply.

Just as 'the devil is in the detail' sometimes it is searching for precision and accuracy that reveals the unexpected. Ideas often escape us that are only a tiny bit different from the normal: even shaving legs is worth doing for the Tour de France. Speaking of legs, when a logging horse pulls trees out of the forest, he is not really pulling from his shoulders so much as pushing with his powerful hind legs. Once you notice this, you see why he can do what a tractor can't.

7. Being resourceful with nothing

In the prisoner of war camps in Germany 1939–45, escape teams were highly ingenious because they had (almost) no resources, for instance to forge passports, dig tunnels, conceal the spoil, make German uniforms, etc. Though many men were in fact recaptured, it's amazing how many did succeed in escaping. *At the same time, but in The Netherlands, a young doctor, Willem Kolff, was ingeniously building the first kidney dialysis machine.* The beauty is not only in his invention but in what he had to make it out of: re-cycling all manner of parts of airplanes, motorcars, tin cans, a bath and sausage skins. He even managed heroically to evade his own dyslexia, went on to create the artificial heart, worked on an artificial eye and ear, and built successful prosthetic arms.

On the other side of the Atlantic, the American engineer and oceanographer John Worzel, who died in 2008, was pioneering sonar. His achievements are almost as astonishing as the fact that, though working with the Navy of a hugely rich nation, he did so much with improvised materials. He is famous for his inventiveness in making practical tools out of commonplace articles, to study the ocean bed. He was working with William Ewing, who, with support from no less a person than President Eisenhower, constructed a camera *using a coffee-can lid for a flash reflector and a thick drinking glass as casing, a seismograph that employed a railroad pocket watch and an oscillograph using the motor from a toy electric train.* Deep-sea explosions were considered impossible but Worzel figured out a way to detonate TNT stuffed into tire inner tubes by using paper caps from toy cowboy revolvers. You couldn't make it up! *"We never allowed ourselves to think that anything we decided to do was impossible,"* he wrote in his 2001 unpublished autobiography.

When a child unwraps a present, s/he might become more interested in its packaging than the present itself. A cardboard box is all sorts of things to a child; she may know what it is for, but what else is it? What is it made of? How do all its features make it work, and what else could they do for her? Before long, it is the box that is the child's toy. How on earth do we manage to kill such versatility?

8. Four filters

We have seen that everything we 'know' is the result of how we perceive it, rather than what it actually is. All information comes through the five (or more) senses and their sensitivity is affected by one's motivation at the time. Its files contain not only what we know but also what we believe, and they keep changing around, randomly. Some patterns of experience are luckier than others in attracting new input, and this luck strengthens our habits. The mental pigeonholes we make seem to act rather like magnets, attracting iron filings of new encounters to themselves.

Not only do we recall some items more readily, but also we cannot always tell whether they reflect what we know or what we believe, what is true or false, good or bad, similar or different, easy or hard. They might just be predictions, or even ideas.

These four channels filter what we receive and make their perception special to each individual. This is why no two people who have witnessed a road accident ever report precisely the same story: it is not that they are lying, but simply that what they actually observed has made different impressions on them, because of what they are. This includes their deep values—what if the driver or the victim were of a different nationality? Moreover, whatever we record depends on our sensitivity at that moment: how many sensors are in use, how much power is on, how close we feel to the incident, and how distracted we were.

Figure 10.3. four filters of perception

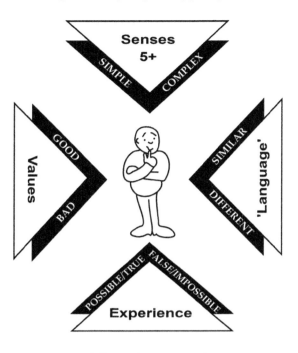

What makes it seem...?
How can I make it seem the opposite?
What 'rules' would be altered?

We all continually create our own experience, subjectively. What happens to me is also filtered by whether I look from a strategic height and long range or for the tactical instant, here and now; the context and what I compare it with; and what I hope for or expect to happen as a result. All these influences whirl around like a kaleidoscope, changing size and shape and sense of order or time.

A. Values: what is 'good'?
Emotional and personal values, which also affect attention and interest, tend to endure in a particular person, but they can also be situational, as whenever you make a decision. *For comfort on a long journey, you favour a large motorcar, whilst for the city you'd prefer a stubby Smartcar.* So 'values' embrace

objectives, aims, motives, criteria, standards, and even instincts and some kinds of feeling. All values color what we experience so much that what is good to one may feel bad to the other. Rusty metal is obviously bad—but can enhance the beauty of sculptures made in a world-famous foundry such as that of Pangolin in Gloucestershire, UK.

Our passions and desires easily over-rule what we receive through our five or more senses, and generally it is impressions that we act upon, rather than the facts. Intensely vivid images naturally rouse emotions more than less immediate ideas, though analogy may be more powerful than direct experience: 'nudes' partly clothed can be more evocative than without anything on at all!

I recall an experiment where people were shown photographs of a man running, followed by a policeman. The man was black and this was America some years ago. The police might of course have been chasing him, but he was actually leading the police to the scene of a fire… Much depends on the images or constructs we hold in our heads. *On a less stark note, weather forecasters have been known to be sorry to predict rain, when actually many farmers and gardeners are praying for it.* There is literally nothing in the world that is in itself entirely 'bad.' *In Nepal, which was once a big sufferer from leprosy, the drug that has done most to reduce the problem is—thalidomide!* With thousands of participants on programs for learning to use more imagination, I have had them think up examples of terrible disasters—and then to find in what ways they could be seen as 'a good thing.' At first it feels impossible, but then haltingly ideas come through, until they become a flood. Needless to say, it works the other way round too: the evils attending 'charity' for instance are legion. *Tragically, it is held by some leading Africans that aid to Africa has done more harm than good to the scope for their building their own future.* Is this also true of the benefits system for the poor and out-of-work in Britain? Or the Accident & Emergency hospital departments, swamped by those who are always getting drunk? The point is, the more counter-intuitive, the more useful it is to identify these often-unconscious constructs or perceptions.

Unusual ideas, whether they turn out to be 'good' or 'bad' for the issue, are clearly at the two extremes of the ideas bell curve: a minority. Once you realize that the middle ground is jostling with competitors, you can bring far more daring versatility to your activities, heedless of the siren voices of 'safety in numbers.' It is all too possible to use one's imagination without being actually creative. New does not mean bad—but it doesn't mean good either, even though one is naturally hoping it will be. It depends where you stand between A, B, C and D in Figure 10.4.

Figure 10.4. Base values

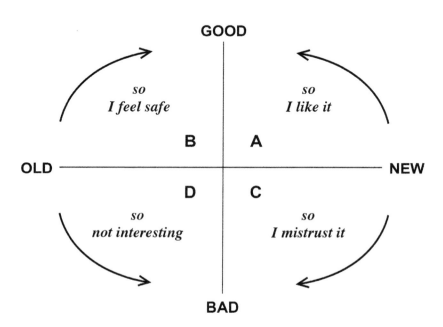

If you impose the disciplines of conceiving only a 'good' idea, you will never stretch beyond what you already know to be good, what is familiar already, or what others are expected to approve of. It is only a truce that we make with our judgment, in order to reach for something different: only temporary. Thinking imaginatively is not a silly thing to do, it is just that no invention can occur so long as everyone sticks to what has been thought or done before. Normally, one's own judgment steps in very early to put a stop to any innovation; an idea needs a chance to live, like a baby when first born, so it's wiser to find out more about it before axing it. Yes is <u>not</u> the opposite of No, which is the killer.

B. 'Language'—is the medium the message?

A second filter is language. How far you go along with Marshall McLuhan on his profound question makes a big difference to how you receive or send any communication. The language or code is just the form or vehicle, but it affects what we 'get' beyond mere words, labeling with symbols, maps, media, models and even number. Birthdays, anniversaries and centuries are examples of how we have given meaning to periods that really have little valid significance. *To score 98 at cricket is brilliant, but such a disappointment*—only because we measure in centuries. Even simple words like 'near' or 'far' need context: how far is Rome? Is it farther for a walker or a Protestant?!

- We fix the person as a car-driver or a passenger, yet he is often a pedestrian.
- In the same way the notion of 'profit' is usually stuck fast to the maker or seller of the product or service, ignoring the 'profit' made by the user or buyer, though this is (hopefully or usually) many times larger.
- The real value of a product or service entails for how many years it continues to provide benefit to the purchaser. It is often this which separates what is bought by the poorer and the richer members of society and perpetuates the gulf between them.
- How different, really, are chalk and cheese?
- Do we enjoy a National Health Service in England or a national sickness service?
- Was this man a terrorist or a freedom fighter?
- Can there be a proper 'war' against terrorism and is it possible to 'win' it?
- Is 'academic' a term of respect or of abuse?

Further examples are legion:

- A cafe, pub, cruise ship, restaurant and hotel could all belong in the same category as providers of catering; but in terms of duration, the cafe, pub and restaurant would come together as short-term, the hotel and ocean liner both provide long-term sleep, and the former are different from the latter. None is a shop.
- Airports make more money from retail shopping than from aircraft. Ryanair, a most profitable airline, makes more from charging for luggage than for your flight.

- Supermarkets can make more by charging suppliers for shelf-space than from selling goods cheaply.
- Companies often re-appraise what kind or aspect of business they wish to be, and change their strategy. When Rolls-Royce realized they did not produce motorcars, but engines, they branched out into the aero industry by founding a quite different company. Then they noticed they were a force in the provision of power, so they formed a special division for that.

What makes anything <u>seem</u> similar/different or good/bad or easy/difficult, etc.? How or in terms of what can I make it seem the other? What is the smallest, most subtle change that could accomplish that? How about the most dramatic? What assumed rules would have to change?

In sum, Marketing is forever seeking new areas in which their company can feel it offers some unique advantage, and this is essentially a creative process fuelled by imagination.

Again, one can ask people to think of two things that are as different from each other as they can possibly imagine—and then ask them to generate in how many ways they are similar. See chalk and cheese above: as with sugar, we all eat an awful lot of chalk! It is astonishing to most people how long is their <u>second</u> list. Naturally, what is already in our experience acts as a sensor or looking glass for new arrivals: is that like this or not? *This is how our immune system works, rejecting some alien virus, or even an organ transplant.* No wonder we are set up to reject anything alien or new to our minds. So when we seek an original solution, we muster energy to get around our own mental immunity defenses.

Significantly, the language made of words engages the rational side of the brain more, while the language of pictures taps the resources of the imaginative side. One trick is to treat words more like pictures when we need more imagination; analogy and metaphor do just that.

C. Easy or difficult?
The distinguished scientist Lord Kelvin, who died in 1907, declared there was no future in radio waves. Yet the same man could envision enormous areas of

physics to be discovered from the rigorous study of molecules! The question whether to open or close the mind now depends on whether you see the situation as 'easy' or 'difficult'; this depends in turn on the standards you apply and the depth of vision. We all have met the fool who thinks something is easy and the high performer who sees the same thing as difficult.

Finding what it is that makes a task difficult is the chief clue to making it easy, for now you know what has to change, or be viewed from a different angle. A characteristic of ingenuity is not to think something <u>is</u> easy, but rather to revel in any difficulty because of being sure it's possible to <u>make it</u> easy. We hold so many experiences that they have formed into clusters, which churn up and down and around, sometimes splitting up and re-forming into new patterns. Scissors might become a lever—or a dagger (therefore forbidden on aircraft). These patterns attract new information to themselves, largely by chance, because of their mobility, but those pathways trodden most often become highways of skill and habit. Equally, the top seeds in tennis tournaments can even lose in the early rounds, as in Wimbledon 2013, because they failed to realize it might not be so easy to walk all over this unknown upstart.

Control is not the same as balance: it offers freedom to risk. Some of the ways used to seek ideas on demand can be seen as akin to madness because when being creative, we extend our experience beyond its normal reach. You are encouraged to push the envelope, go out on a limb, reach to extremes. Moreover, as soon as someone thinks up an original idea, all unoriginal people know he is wrong, so courage is a must.

D. Is it fact or belief? Can we say it is true or false?
It can be hard to tell the difference between fact and belief, but it's no use to argue with facts unless they are irrelevant, because they have to be true. Most of the time, any new ideas that come to light are ignored, belittled or savagely obliterated by the majority of other people. Beliefs are a matter of opinion, so might be true or false, and it is worth knowing the intentions of the person uttering them. What is he trying to reach for with his mind? Any idea that is 'new' is bound to violate or differ from what is already known and/or believed. An incalculable number of ideas die in the throat, which later turn out to be successful, and we live to regret our caution. History is full of great ideas with difficult launches.

After all, everything, including the moon, has its other side—it is only our position that hides it from our telescope. *If you live in California, is the Far East to the west?* So we can always force out new perceptions by asking, "In terms of what are we viewing this?" Dead flowers make excellent decoration—or compost.

'Rapid cycling' is the name given to describe what Mozart could do: almost simultaneously cycle from high joyous to low sad. You need special motivation to toggle between the dual faces of these four filters, pretending something is simple instead of complex, bad instead of good, similar instead of different, false instead of true—and vice versa all round. This demands we be agile and flexible enough with our senses, our emotions, our categories and our means of expression. Then we can embrace this duality to see things anew—or to see something new altogether.

IV
Allow wonder and imagination

Chapter 11
Allow Yourself Anything

Allow yourself to wonder. The key attitude is to let everything enter your mind, yes anything. Make yourself so malleable that nothing jars, and jettison all the rules and experience that resist whatever won't fit your familiar facts and beliefs. Give space, for more than a moment, to intuition and gut feel, being open even to a touch of magic and your instincts for inspiration. It can always be justified as 'the unexplained so far.'

1. Welcome all and any ideas

What does creativeness mean? Until recently, the word had not even appeared in dictionaries. Yet today everyone is so concerned to be creative that it is in danger of becoming a motherhood word. Some people see advertising agencies as full of 'creative' people and production managements empty of them. Others look to the marketing or training departments, seeing work study or accounting as their polar opposites. Privately owned businesses tend to feel themselves more creative than governmental bureaucracies, and those who found small entrepreneurial outfits have often left a large organization where it had been impossible to pursue their brilliant idea. *Even Rolls-Royce allowed Sir David McMurtry and John Deer to leave in 1973 and develop their probe for extremely accurate 3D measurement of the inside of the Concorde aero engine: they founded their own company, Renishaw plc, now among world leaders in metrology.* Some years ago, it was calculated that in the USA 60% of new products came about this way, perhaps because huge organizations don't easily embrace change.

They may not give permission to stretch further along each of the two vectors of the Relevance Box, reaching towards the most remote and most unlikely possibilities. The key attitude needed is that anything is allowed, all and everything.

Figure 11.1. the dreamer (Cecil William Rhodes)

2. Undoing the familiar

To adopt a new idea, you have to throw away something of the old one. Entering this wider world is so much easier when you simply go flexible in your mind. We are used to this in our body, especially if we have engaged in sport, the performing arts or hand-to-hand combat.

- Modeling with clay demands you make it warm and malleable.
- Making a mock-up is easier with wire than with cast iron.
- You teach your child to float in the water, not by stiffening and struggling out of fear, but from giving herself to the bosom of the ocean, knowing it doesn't matter to keep her head up because actually she won't sink.
- In the fairground there are bumper-cars, whose whole point is to throw out the normal traffic rules, or else you are behaving like a maiden aunt.

Abandon those rigid categories by which we order our lives efficiently. Let go all our oughts. Embrace becoming slippery and ambiguous instead of being firm, consistent and reliable. How would a designer manage without a pencil that could be rubbed out? Indian ink is fine for the final drawing, but not at the beginning or on the way there—think how great it is that our computer lets us be infinitely free to change it on screen without consequence.

In the workshops I run inside companies for producing new concepts and inventions, instead of the flipchart and easel I often get everyone writing their thoughts on small pieces of card, stickies or even scraps of paper, so that they don't feel the angst of commitment in the moment. Small chits can readily be moved around, connected to something else, put in a group of similar thoughts, or put on the back-burner, even crumpled and thrown away. What freedom! With such freed space, shared by all, other people feel encouraged to attach their own comments, and take advantage of even an idea that's not much good at first but can be developed. The whole purpose is to allow and enable one to postpone making judgments that might kill an idea stone dead, before its potential has been realized.

Let's learn from other people's ideas as well as our own, because nothing is carved in stone anymore. We all have permission to be as rude and cavalier as we need, to be utterly spontaneous. When politeness and good manners have been suspended for the moment, it's amazing to notice how being careful had slowed things down. As it is, whatever is ejaculated is immune from either criticism or the taking of offense. Most of us have heard someone say "I'm only thinking out loud" so as to excuse whatever might sound like rubbish and expose them as an idiot. We need more idiotic thoughts, especially as the reaction to them may produce a winner.

The single most powerful stride you can take to find new or exceptional ideas is simply to get yourself into the right frame of mind—widen out, as a physical coach will say. Symbolically, you put on your creative hat, announcing to anyone nearby, and not least to yourself, that you are now operating in a world of fantasy, where all the rules are different, as if in paradise or a child's fairy story.

This may not be as easy as it seems, for normal life requires ordinary critical thinking to test wild suppositions for reliability. Under pressure we have learned to live taut, with stiffened sinews in case of attack. The wisdom of experience teaches to conform with the norms of our group, and to take only calculated risks. It is hard to open ourselves out, to let go of almost everything we know and believe; it is not only difficult but also seen as wrong. Programmed activity drives out unprogrammed activity—so you'd better program some time each day to do nothing! It's hard to do this unless or until you work for yourself.

Ideas are threatening, not only to the current wisdom but also to those who hold it. 'I haven't spent all these years of study and research just to find it all overturned by some new 'discovery.' The defensiveness aroused then readily turns into attack; worse still, the attack is made not only on the heresy but also on the 'heretic.' You have to first address these spontaneous natural fears, else you have a fight on your hands which you will probably lose—and the probability goes UP the better your new idea is! Clearly there are far reaching implications here for the waging of a campaign to innovate an invention.

Figure 11.2. an open hand (Cecil William Rhodes)

Show an open hand. Unless you allow your mind to be wide open to any-thing, pliable, shapeless, and free from any particular direction or structure, anything really unusual that comes onto your horizon will be left unnoticed or ignored. It will not fit what is already there. When brainstorming or gen-erating a whole lot of ideas, deep habits of numbering thoughts or trying to think of them in a sensible sequence have to be abandoned, *pro tem*. They reduce and constrain what you produce with freedom—but so many people do not realize this yet. Much better to make a more random 'map' or develop a spidergram where you can slot in thoughts from a variety of directions. It could even be that ideas have some energy of their own, and will not even swim into your periphery if they sense you would not welcome them. What a ridiculous thought, some reader might gasp. Well, there you are: if you aren't willing even to entertain a ridiculous idea for more than a moment, it won't stand a chance. The sting in this tail is that most of the truly outstanding achievements in every field of life have encountered instant rejection at first sight.

Figure 11.3. visionary joy

3. A feeling in my water

When we are blessed with an insight, it often feels like a shaft of light from the heavens or a soaring leap upwards to somewhere special. With a rational abstraction, you can explain how it came about, but it's possible to make an intuitive connection without enough reasoned evidence.

> *"Intuition is the immediate insight into truth*
> *that comes when we grasp a proposition and its*
> *proof in a single act of mental attention."*
>
> ROGER SCRUTON ON SPINOZA

This means the idea is at risk, and only some ideas survive the test of proof, but by throwing discipline to the winds, one can seize the high ground with amazing speed. This form of imagination is capable of initiating 80% of results in only 20% of the time, but usually we don't give it the chance.

Gut feel entails that you welcome, listen for and entertain such intuitions— especially when they are not justified! Scientists, unlike the general public, treat all their own findings and conclusions as a matter of probability, assuming a certain degree of error; they are not so naive as to believe they ever discover an absolute, universal and eternal 'fact.' Yet the best may well resort to an apparently unrespectable way to reach verity: to go beyond normal perceptions, listening to their own sensing of a new idea, and allowing it to survive its birth. It is certainly a contentious way to escape 'accepted knowledge,' though Albert Einstein, a scientist famous for his respect for intuitions, wrote, "He who is certain of the truth is shipwrecked by the laughter of the gods…" Of course our mentors continue to intone that sound thought requires facts and some tangible expression of something observed, heard, tasted, smelt or physically felt. The evidence-based mantra conjoins with the demand to quote sources in an academic paper to assure that nothing new can reasonably be entertained, so candidates usually play it safe. All this provokes the tease that "This doesn't work in theory: only in practice." So which do you believe in enough to act on it?

Intuition requires high confidence in one's own exercise of this faculty, and it is interesting that our database on the *Rhodes' Thinking-Intentions Profile* shows it is a thinking preference most 'allowed' among very senior executives. (Perhaps less senior people don't dare, in case they are not promoted!) I did establish there was reality in the speculation of a client of mine in Shell, namely that whenever someone rises above a certain level in the organization, they begin to believe in their own inklings. In the British military, this level is somewhere near the point where you 'get egg on your cap'—Commander Royal Navy, Colonel, Wing Commander Royal Air Force. Titles in business are less obvious, but most of us knew it when reaching the level where we could feel liberated! Decision-making, especially on strategic issues, is done using intimations more than many laymen might think. Top executives can feel it is actually respectable for wise people like themselves to behave more like entrepreneurs!

The 'sixth sense' feels rather like scribing a perfect curve or circle by hand: a tacit skill which, like catching a ball, is naturally learned rather than taught. *One looks back to Giotto's O in the Middle Ages, or Royce's ability to make the single large hexagon wheel-nut for the Rolls motorcar, by hand.* (Try it!) I do believe in intuition, and always urge people not to ignore it but rather to listen longer and consider its implications more seriously. It is by definition unjustifiable, at least in theory though not in practice. Ultimately we did find out how the bumblebee achieves the 'impossible' and actually does fly.

"Any sufficiently advanced technology is
indistinguishable from magic."
ARTHUR C CLARKE,
PROFILES OF THE FUTURE, 1961

More often than we do so, it would be worth venturing into areas just out of reach of observation. When you come with a proposal to spend time and money on some new idea or project, your superior requires a case to be made for it, and will send you back to do your homework before s/he will even consider it. And yet, and yet... Who has not bitterly regretted ignoring the danger signals about some person, against one's 'better judgment'? I also plead guilty: it's common to recruit someone who ticked all the boxes and to ignore those signs, only to find out later he or she is a disaster. Isn't it interesting we say I *felt* that was an opportunity, or I *smelt* a rat?

Most adults accept there is more in what we see than meets the eye, even with the inner eye. The American artist Hopper said recently, "If I could say it in words, I wouldn't have to paint it." We often stretch out our hands and minds to take in thoughts we cannot really understand. You have to listen to any suspicion of a glimpse, when it speaks to your inner ear. The entrepreneur is familiar with his 'hunch,' and so are the good scientist, the inventor, the artist (of all kinds) and the person who produces a film or show. "I think I have a painting coming on"—or a novel, a play or a symphony. But it happens to us all. Kant wrestled with notions that cannot be observed through the five senses.

Pasteur said, "Fortune favors the prepared mind" so there is a genuine tension between those who belong to the 'magical' school and those who are more like a craftsman. The latter, faced with the conflict between the wildness of imagination and the ascetic soundness of logic, will seek some rationale which has to optimize it.

Maybe inspiration too comes to a prepared mind. By the way, I use the word 'intuition' to mean something different from the famous intuition of women, which is more a matter of close and deep observation of what is going on, as distinct from knowledge-without-fact, which is available just as much to men. I roughly remember a description made by Charles Dickens: *I feel there is a pain in the room somewhere, but what and where it is I cannot begin to say!*

A feeling in my water has not yet been destroyed by 'civilization,' education or social mores: it is akin to 'star quality,' whether in footballers, scientists or film stars. This seems a little like resonance: powerful frequencies that cannot otherwise be recorded. It may feel ephemeral and elusive—but it exists all right and often works, not only in the entertainment industry, where it is a make-or-break factor and is paid for with a long string of noughts. In the 1960s, I tried without success to nail it for Rank Films, Rank Audio Visual and Pinewood Studios. We don't know much about how it operates, but I wonder if there could be some connection with instincts, properly so called. Deep in the reptilian brain, there remain some kinds of reflex that help us survive by sending instant signals for movement that do not apparently depend on thought. *By the firing of his colliculi, the basketball player can place the ball into the net with his eyes tight shut.* This seems to be more directive than the autonomic systems that keep us breathing, for example. Could it be something like these 'instincts' that warn us of the motorcar in front, which is positioned to go left but will actually turn right?

Sadly, we have all been trained to over-rule these perceptions on 'scientific' grounds. But some scientists read them as 'the unexplained so far.' What if a budding genius came up with a new but profound proposition in his exam paper or thesis? It would be treated as rubbish. Perhaps we should at least give hunches the space to breathe and live and develop, before we evaluate and dismiss them. The brain represents 2% of body mass but uses 20% of energy—to produce 80% of Results. The African who crafted the axe discovered in the Rift Valley was not officially an engineer, but he understood this leverage 1.6 million years ago.

Chapter 12
The Power of IF

Making suppositions of what (only) might be true seems to take second place to what can be proven to be so, yet it is a vital skill for uncovering what we need to know and also discovering the potential future. Children pretend, adults simulate and develop scenarios of what if .... were to happen? Two core questions for every situation we face are 'What might have caused this?' and 'What might this cause?' They drive the imagination to find the answers for judgment, including predicting and interpreting. Curiosity is another 'mental instinct' or intentional quest, whose strong suit is questioning and favourite phrase 'what else?' So many have lost this skill since childhood and no longer take any trouble to learn.

1. Just pretend

The small word, *if*, packs a huge punch. It opens out a world of what might be true, what you suppose, what you wonder. When a solution is not there, your only choice is to pretend it might be. This innocent word means to create hypotheses, without having to believe in them. As children in our land of wonder, everything is allowed. But also adults—the current advertising for Sony carries this very strap line: "Make believe." Of course grown-ups imagine what it would be like to have the shiny and advanced new product in their home; they are always thinking up what they could do if they or their situation were different. *What if I won the lottery?*

Applying this to getting ideas, we can treat first thoughts as loss leaders—not profitable in themselves but inviting something that might be so. The problem still remains that adults are encouraged to 'put away childish things' and stick with discipline applied to reasoned facts. So in most businesses around the world, the concept of developing scenarios of the (possible) future was by no means common practice, and has only grown widespread since Shell's pioneering work around 1970. In fact the Anglo-Dutch energy giant attributed their successful handling of the oil crisis in that decade to having developed scenarios of worst case, optimistic and most likely futures, and so were better able to handle the crisis when it materialized.

Figure 12.1. if only

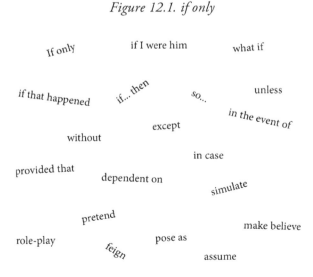

What if your perceptions or interpretation of events could be wrong or changed? We assume *this* matters because of *that*, but suppose it doesn't? We might be mistaken about what something means.

- Is it obvious that to achieve sustainable world peace, we must bring democracy to all?
- The trend of earnings or populations is to rise, but...
- People today are living longer—does this entail serious health problems being a greater or a lesser burden on society?
- Of course we should send aid to the Third World—unless this will make matters even worse for them.
- Global warming will melt the icecaps, raise ocean levels and make Britain colder.

Anyone can make a long list of such natural conclusions, and we are aware they are not always reliable. However, the point here is to bring out onto the table all the spontaneous thoughts that spring to mind when addressing any issue requiring more imagination than it has received so far. Then to use those possibilities as raw material or ammunition for building on or changing them. It is the natural follow-through from having challenged assumptions.

To pretend is to simulate or role-play. For instance, in designing a revolutionary lawn-mower, what do the blades feel like when cutting a strong weed that appears amid the grass?

Stretch out to the opportunities. Some new solutions are the result of re-alignment between the inner person and their situation. Focusing on the former, try changing your own viewing-point, playing a role. What if we no longer had our car, how could we possibly manage without it? The trick is to be aware you are just playing a game, which you will only temporarily believe in: you know you don't know, so you mustn't be committed to any idea whilst still spawning it. We are all used to trial runs, simulating reality and developing plans based on the most likely forecasting—the English are forced to do this every single day, with their weather in mind! Such mental exercises are more common when thinking up what we might do and what might happen in the <u>world outside</u> us. Here I am suggesting you also do it to yourself, inside. Can you cause yourself to alter your mind-set, to love what

173

you normally hate, to welcome what you normally fear—and vice versa? Rather than building a new airplane, perhaps we could choose values that steered towards less travel?—it might be easier, faster and cheaper. Be aware that we are trying something in the mind by thinking, not yet trying it out for real, which entails risk and expense.

Tricking your own mind in order to uncover a new and useful idea requires not just skill but also motivation. This may involve delving through more than one layer of thought or construct.

When laws produce unintended consequences (as they always do!), whenever life takes us by surprise, we have failed to imagine one of them. If something unplanned does actually happen, what might cause it and therefore what else might have prevented it? If we can think up some preventive measure, how effective could it be, how likely is it to fail, so would it all be worth it? Pursuing further, just <u>how</u> might it fail and if it did, what might lessen the effects or cushion the blow? If we took measures now, in case, how safe do we feel and is it worth buying that insurance? All such possibilities and their branches depend upon the tiny word IF. It helps us govern both the unknown and the future.

2. Curiosity

Curiosity is the gift of every child, who has not yet learned to grow tired of quest. "I wonder what might be inside that, behind it or beyond?" It is driving the glee of hunting the Easter egg in the garden, and it is the question shared with pretty well all puppies and kittens, probably every higher creature. Too often, young people lose their natural curiosity in growing up. From a lifetime of experience, especially of observing how people think, I am still amazed to find so many otherwise able people who seem to have so little curiosity left. They just don't seem to care about stones they leave unturned or opportunities they don't pursue. Offered half-information, they fail to pursue the other half; when triggered with a question left hanging in the air, they do not seize it. This can be so frustrating, especially as nearly all the children I've come across are bursting with curiosity, so much so that as soon as he learns to walk, you have to remove everything within reach! If not, whatever is below four feet will be unscrewed, taken to pieces, tasted, sniffed and destroyed! Oh, and they will find a way to reach higher. It's a perpetual problem, how much rope to give 'em. Even an infant can find out how to use the iPad quicker than me.

But a child is soon told that curiosity killed the cat, that constantly asking "Why?" is irritating, and he puts up his hand too often in class. This is especially so if the teacher cannot give the answer or it's been asked at the wrong moment. The seeking instinct is gradually worn down, cauterized or even extinguished. Too many schools are laying the foundations for the hatred of learning that so many adults now suffer from. All this in a world of innovation and change that has pushed learning up the scale to become one of the most essential skills throughout one's career. How did we ever do without Google?

Figure 12.2. curiosity

"Curiosity is the lust of the mind" (Thomas Hobbes, d. 1679). Curiosity is tireless in its search for anything useful, never satisfied with being short-changed, moving heaven and earth in a sustained line of enquiry. People who are still curious are full of hope, always willing to peel away another layer and pursue any implications. Their strong suit is questioning and their favorite phrase is 'what else?' They are the ones who find all the variations possible because they always feel they are nearly there, they have all but the solution and it will come soon. So they have the energy and stamina to try all

avenues, look for exceptions, and come up with a flow of ideas. Anyone with this degree of motivation who also is armed with suites of questions is a gift for any brainstorm.

"Curiouser and curiouser" (*Alice in Wonderland*). But it does depend on time, and how far and how wide you feel willing to pursue your search outside what might sound reasonable. There is always treasure lying within you that seems forbidden, so that one fails to tap into it. In the driest desert, the deeper you dig, the more water will come. Even more riches lie beyond our current reach, so that one needs to muster the energy to keep on looking for more ideas than one already has.

As Edison famously remarked, "Genius is 1% inspiration and 99% perspiration." But the motivation behind all that sweat may come in two forms.

First, there is the conscientious duty to be analytic and thorough in the drive for precise detail and absolute completeness, because you want to know all there is to know and to marshal it all as well. She asks, "What else IS there?" *Famous or notorious for this, (depending on your point of view) are the civil servant, the administrative clerk, the income tax collector and inspector, the car service mechanic (!), the people who need long lists and tick-boxes.* Being punctilious has real value when it comes to logistics, statistics, appendices, store keeping, accounting, and all kinds of legalistic activities. The phlegmatic mind-set of a stamp-collector bears every mark of exacting diligence, qualities necessary for the successful explorer, though certainly not sufficient. When dispensing medicines, checking for instruments after a surgical operation, counting men down the mine, or counting back aircraft to the carrier, you had better be rigorous and exhaustive. The carpenter cuts once but measures twice.

Oliver Messel, the incomparable designer, learned much from doing that work before he became also a painter and builder of many houses. "I think that the less you know technically, the more is known. Your mind must imagine first, then get over the technical difficulties." For the scenery of "The Magic Flute" opera staged at Glyndebourne, he made no fewer than 800 sketches.

Second, there is the energy of hope, that by exploring much wider and longer than is normal, I will generate many, many ideas and one of them might deliver the prize I seek. He asks, "What else <u>MIGHT</u> there be?," inviting questions of speculation: what could be beyond the visible, and how could it possibly be extended? This looks for exceptions, unusual implications, things hidden within. It often draws on optimistic disclaimers such as 'so far,' 'usually' or 'nearly'; *Professor Dole, who famously showed how smoking was the cause of lung cancer, probably said "among other factors."* And a skeptic could say 'as yet,' renewable energy is not the solution we seek. This is the energy of a restless search, seeming quick to change direction but with nose relentlessly on the scent. To this end, the Imagineer will use every trick in the book of the exacting reductionist. He will find shades of subtle meaning, sail close to the wind, exploit a description to its utmost extremes, and carry on for as long as it takes to come up with a new idea. Instead of gathering all the information that is known to be needed, he reaches for everything not-yet-known, that *might be.* Some of the skills are held in common with the pernickety: but the intent or <u>attitudes</u> are poles apart.

3. Managing two kinds of perseverance

In this vein, the Imagineer is empowered to take everything either to extremes beyond what is normally reasonable, or with a large pinch of salt. Fluent, fertile and versatile, the more he pursues more ideas the more he raises his chance of finding a good one. When panning for gold, the more times you dip into the river, the more tiny flecks you will find. He has *carte blanche*, and is totally immune to any form of criticism from either Feelers or Reasoners. This is because the Imagineer's goal or role has to be different if he is to supply the needs of the other two. This is not the evidence that something is right; nor the feel for what is good; but rather the potential for something new. Needless to say this is addressing the need, not necessarily a want. He is simply seeking ideas, options and solutions that *might* turn out to be exceptionally successful but have not yet been thought of. He has to be fluent and fertile, thinking up more ideas in minutes than ordinary people would even try for. To be any better, those ideas must be significantly novel, so probably the outcome of something unorthodox in his approach. *When a golfer is stuck in a difficult bunker and every shot fails to get him onto the green, only the stupid one keeps using the same stroke:* the master might even take hold of a different club altogether. The Cool part of the Imagineer's role is to get you out of impossible situations, or to win on impossible tasks. This is done through intense ingenuity and resourcefulness.

When it comes to research, businesses and governments alike often face the issue of whether to fund 'blue sky' research, pursuing curiosity and exploring further how the world works, without a specific objective in mind. Thus, seeking a cure for cancer or diabetes is felt more purposeful and worthy than finding out how biological cells work. Yet this is to ignore the dual reason for research: the first is to discover 'what would be good for that?'; the second is to realize 'what could this be good for?' We have only to consider how few and narrow were the perceived uses for the computer or the laser at first: since then, applications for both are multiplying every week. Imagine the caveman needing to move a boulder, who placed a stone near it, and wedged in a branch. Aha! A lever is a tool to move boulders... Is that all a lever can do? Are boulders all it can move? When you've caught a crab or a lobster for dinner, is your only tool for reaching the meat a sharp stone?

Figure 12.3. how else?

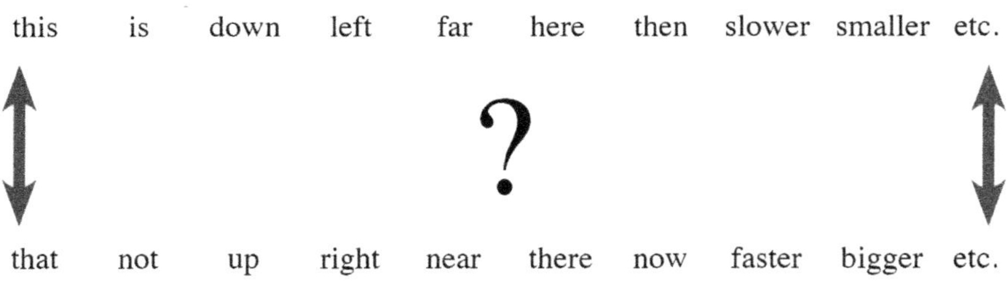

this	is	down	left	far	here	then	slower	smaller	etc.
↕				**?**					↕
that	not	up	right	near	there	now	faster	bigger	etc.

The next great trend of innovation will be not so much of new products, though that will continue, but rather of social values. The influence of phenomena like Jugaad Innovation from India, the Ubislate tablet for the masses and micro finance to poor people challenges the Western notion of 'better is better' and brings another face of 'Small is Beautiful' to some of the most sophisticated companies in the world.

Very creative people, those whose wild ideas actually work, approach with a kind of controlled duality, directing emphasis towards either wild fantasy or cold blue logic. The key 'must' is never trying to do both at once. One must choose between ranging abroad for game to hunt or cutting down the harvest. Like a fisherman, the Imagineer knows when to launch forth the nets for ideas and when to haul in the catch. Like a financier, he balances the expansion of his portfolio with timely profit taking, monitoring his activities, deciding when the solutions generated need evaluation, now, before generating more. This central function of control enables one to explore randomly and without sequential dependence or some routine order of thought dictated by a textbook. Control over the 'central nervous system' of our thought will remain more rare than it should, until more people adopt a conscious methodology for thought, with the skill to recognize the kind of thinking going on and the kind that should be!

Our Cool analytical mind has to overcome severe restraints before it will allow imagination full rein. But I try to make the logical case for becoming free from constraints when this is required. It is then easier to reconcile an astonishing idea with whatever people are normally used to: otherwise, the new idea gets bogged down in resistance, or rejected outright. Reason works only when you have the information: what is special about creating new ideas is that information is precisely what you haven't got. Normal channels for seeking it were not working, so you turned to unusual channels. This works best when the frontal lobes are shut down for a while because they are our guardians and inhibitors. Creativity is not a linear process, like a factory, where every thinking element or skill must be used, usually in the right order, for a successful product to emerge.

An idea might actually be reached just by being curious enough to seek the unusual.

Chapter 13
Simply Connect

Many a brilliant idea has come from seeing the similarity or abstract connection between things normally seen as remote from each other: the wider the stretch, the more improbable, the better. It's often how you re-frame a logical category, picturing another relationship by suggestion in the unconscious mind. The unifying simplicity of a new idea comes from the fusion between converging in on an abstraction and diverging out to a connection, best done by analogy and picturing. It's as if you produce new spectrums or dimensions or criteria out of a hat – and then even cross-reference them! To multiply your images faster than adding them, think in holograms. Vision can create a magnetic force-field, that attracts ideas through some kind of fellow-feeling with your goal.

1. The art of Abstraction has two faces

Many ideas come from purely logical abstraction. Man, who apparently can think only at about 120 thought-images per second, keeps ahead of the exponentially faster computers he develops, by a number of useful tricks that give him or her phenomenal short cuts. Making patterns from known facts is one, and we see the world as infinite hierarchies of parts of wholes, kinds of other kinds, stages of longer phases, causes of effects.

Suppose you name your concern as X.
Then ask, is X a part of a larger concern, called y?
But does y have concerns comparable with X?
If so, focus on the comparator of X, and if not probe X deeper
Does the most crucial part of your chosen concern have its own concerns?'
Now from all these, which is your priority?

y

x   X   x

z z z z z z z

The beauty is, this trick applies to <u>kinds</u> of concern, and <u>stages</u> of a plan as well. So each of the three can be seen as the TRUNK of a tree with its own roots and branches.

Figure 13.1. roots and branches of thought

Secondly, we all dance to the tune of similarity and difference, connect and disconnect. In a busy cloakroom, I may easily recognize my own coat because I can discern its difference from the others. But suppose it were the cloakroom for a top floor restaurant that had caught fire. Now, to escape to the ground below, I have to invent some ingenious way down that may need an entirely different notion of similarities. What things can I see that could make a rope?—scarves, sleeves, curtains, sash cords are all long, strong and knottable enough to become similar. Everything can be used outside its proper purpose, and the trick is to find the abstract new purpose, which is rather a 'virtual' quality that you conceive in the eye of the mind, a connection that works. A little like alchemy—and simplicity.

Even higher animals, including humans, have great difficulty in making or following abstractions—though even the fruit fly can do it a bit. 'I cannot count oranges, only apples.' When Daddy counts the stairs whilst taking his child up to bed, he is hoping she will be learning how to count her dolls and toys and everything else. So often, the more simple the outward face, the more complex the guts inside. If I meet someone halfway <u>up</u> the mountain, could he have already been to the top so that he is now halfway <u>down</u>? This would make his position different.

What justifies treating tomatoes as fruit, rather than vegetables? What do fruits have in common that separates them all from vegetables—is it to do with sweetness versus savory and would you be tempted by potatoes—which belong to the same family? It is even an act of imagination to think up which items are to be left outside one's definition of 'fruit,' for some things will be more 'significant by their absence' than others. How about beechnuts, or blossom? So imagination must play a role even in the differentiation needed for stark logic.

To speak of 'discrimination' these days is apparently not politically correct, yet it is a hallmark of the human being. How could our civilization have grown without the discovery of formulae, equations, and laws of physics and jurisprudence? Man has even attempted the secret of beauty, with rules of contrast, line, shape and function. A classical example is the Golden Section, dividing the length of a line into two so that the lesser is 0.382 and the longer 0.618. This unique proportion, giving 1:1.618, can be multiplied indefinitely and also offers a running series of numbers whose increase is constant, so that each succeeding number is equal to the sum of the previous two. Wow! Over the two millennia since the discovery of the Golden Section, a host of further such brilliant insights have enriched and accelerated our lives.

The interaction between Order and Chaos in conceiving a new idea reminds one of some kind of helical DNA chain, a lemniscate or the Moebius strip. It's all a matter of intention, reminding us of the interaction between emotion and intelligence seen in Chapter 8.

Figure 13.2. order and chaos lemniscate

2. Just connect

How on earth can I make ideas come? I believe that insightful patterns come from making extra-ordinary connections, forming a <u>relationship</u> that suddenly matters, sometimes between things so remote as to be barely seen to exist. This is the closest we get to 'creating.' This is what Homo sapiens, wise or thinking Man, exploits when he forms whatever he faces into some picture, for images offer so many ways to interpret them. Any old remote association won't do, else it won't work and most 'normal' thinkers won't follow, but remember that a <u>good</u> idea violates logic only at first sight. Find the special conditions that justify it, for all you need is a hint, a whisper, just a glimpse. It helps to feel some empathy with mystery, hidden or latent meaning, so there's a natural welcome for implications, connotations, affinities, synonyms and the symbolism of language. Whilst Reason demands that things you are connecting do connect, imagining anything new allows you to say <u>perhaps</u> they might, and your connection can begin as quite fleeting or bizarre. Elusive constructs are reached by suggestion, engaging the unconscious mind, scorning the literal, and embracing a variety of ways to describe something that might reveal some unity.

How could one think of the proposal to extract sunlight from cucumbers! (Jonathan Swift's *Gulliver's Travels*). Was this the first idea for reverse engineering—or for the ground source heat pump we enjoy today? It has recently been said that thought is simply condensed light and that an atom is just a sheath for the spirit within it (Howard Smith). Could we store light, or weigh sunshine? Is light a noun or a verb, and if it is a thing, what happened to the light in my room when I closed the door? How did Newton and Leibniz 'get an idea' like calculus? What about WIMP: Weakly Interacting Massive Particles? Such notions capture and represent both abstract qualities and the quality of things. It is our way to connect something invisible, intangible or 'spiritual' with something more material.

Ideas are fluid and slippery, and may come with reluctance or at the speed of light. Like the eagle, ideas need no roads and the logic of their connections comes only afterwards, when seen to work. The neurons in the right brain apparently have more branches than those in the left, enabling them to collect ideas that are widely different and therefore make novel connections.

Some time in childhood, everyone wakes up to the realization that his or her view of the world is not the only one—I remember exactly where I was, under a cedar tree and I was eight, when this great truth dawned on me! Once over this threshold, respect for other people's views and sensible discussion is much easier. But this is not enough. If we examine just how anyone <u>might</u> describe what they experience, a great new world of wonder opens up in a practical way.

The secret is to go beyond organizing the facts we have, to envision something <u>not</u> in sight, making something out of nothing. Who was who said "*We'd never have discovered electric light if we'd done all our Research & Development on a candle."*? Instead of being evidence-bound or constipated, we should look very hard at the nature of guesswork, and not treat the concept in a pejorative way, but realize its value for original thought and how a guess is brought through as an insight. Not all speculations are proven wrong, but small wonder it took 100 years to prove Einstein right on gravitational waves.

3. Symbolic unity and simplicity

Reach in for abstractions, reach out for connections. We are reminded of Liam Hudson's Divergers and Convergers. The key to the apparent tension between the two kinds of thought is that one cannot do one without the other, as with Man and Woman. The question is, which has the upper hand now, which is driving the other, as scissors or shears depend on one blade bearing against the other. Whilst reason without imagination is barren, imagination without reason may not work. Mathematics itself is the sublime conjunction of both.

Some years ago, I was engaged by Philips in a project to explore the fundamental processes entailed in conceiving new products. Also involved were four of the most outstanding inventors in the organization, perhaps among the best in Europe or the world. One conclusion we reached was that when the opposing powers of logical reason and symbolic imagination are forced together, they produce this blinding flash. Something we know, we see dramatically anew: or else we realize something new altogether. This fusion is as Greek meets Greek: no wonder it brings such a rush of blood to the head.

Since ideas cannot easily be expressed physically, we symbolize or do it by suggestion and metaphor. Though everyone may not get the message, it is just what is needed to stimulate new ideas, especially with someone else. Any kind of analogy also bridges the needs of aesthetics and originality. By their nature, images can represent many meanings at once, some implicitly, others explicitly. The secret is to realize that when one thinks something to be impossible, it might only be the rigid or narrow use of reason making it so: as if the biggest object had to be the heaviest—all things equal, it ought to be, surely? Symbolic imagination widens the paradigm almost infinitely, to discover the conditions required for the biggest to actually be the lightest of all. Think of a cast iron block standing on an ice-covered lake: what happens to its 'weight' if we attach a rope and whirl it around? As David Hume remarked: "If used more than ordinarily freely and widely this (symbolic) interpretation of experience is what constitutes genius" (genius is from Latin *gignere* to beget). The simplicity of an insight can feel sublime and almost mystical or spiritual.

Analogy provokes or lets in a new perception. Just consider how many ways the tree has been used for various concepts. There are always other ways to achieve something than those we already know. A way to reach more of them is to think up options that are different but analogous, however subtle the similarity or tenuous the link. Metaphor can meld together notions that are impossibly far apart, just as the skillful communicator uses parables and examples to get around opposition. In fact to reach a special insight, exploit the power of symbolism to unite two concepts otherwise seen as remote. The more wide apart they are, the more chance of an outstanding insight.

An enormous proportion of our language is in fact some form of 'image,' so that to treat things too literally can be so incongruous it is often the device of a joke. I doubt if the temperature of her brain dropped when "she looked at him coldly" but we have an idea how she feels, and suffer with him accordingly. Our memory has thousands of such constructs, most of which we have never mined. Pick up any popular newspaper, one not restricted to the most able, intelligent or creative people, and you will find, even in the headlines, words used that have bridged eons of space between the event and its description there in print. Yet clearly the message reaches readers of *The Sun* and *The Mirror or the so-called 'gutter press'*. Those crack journalists in the 'red-tops' glory in them, and have found a new continuum, a new dimension, perhaps a new 'conceptual sense'? It is of course called a metaphor. On an old paper that was lining a drawer, I found the following headlines, all in one issue:

- Vaccine victims win Round 1
- The case of the blue film
- Gormley raps rebels
- Brazil snatches victory
- Wales draw, but lose the war
- Historic marriage of Calamity Jane and Bobby Jones [they turn out to be golf clubs]
- Paul the Revivalist sets out on his mission [the Davis Cup]
- Amis is struck by lightning [a cricket ball]

Sub-editors achieve in words what the cartoonist delivers in drawings: emotional impact, humor and intellectual delight. Their readers receive a magical extra meaning or excitement from such headlines and their jokes, even in the sporting pages. But imagery works also for serious thought: analogies do not merely express and convey something strongly, they add a new angle and change the meaning of what you know, bringing insight on the wings of surprise.

A thought knows no physical bounds at all, save the need to reconcile abstraction with reality, and the energy to explore all conceivable directions.

4. We see the world through dimensions

Both critical thinking and common sense seem to operate on a flat plane made by the two dimensions of knowledge and reason. Bringing in another dimension enables you to see the flat earth from up in the heavens, to change your field of vision or the level of your categories. This means you can see more sharply in a narrow arc or envision more widely from a greater height. Shell calls this faculty 'Helicopter' and identified it as one of four characteristics needed for higher management. One can still think with super-effectiveness <u>inside</u> the box, by enlarging the scope of the box.

In the simplest example, in the designing and training of a robot, it has to learn how to move, and the three spatial dimensions, vertical up/down, lateral left/right and forward/back enable you to position any point in space, precisely and without argument. This also means you can make any object of any shape, even print layer upon layer of two-dimensional material to become three-dimensional, as in 'additive manufacturing' today. By changing even one dimension, you can produce a new shape.

What if you were to extend your dimensions beyond the obvious one of space and time, and therefore motion? How about extent? And mass? And energy? Combinations of such dimensions spawn others still, like speed or force or direction. And they have sub-elements such as light and weight and texture, interval, regularity and rhythm, resonance, contrast and balance. Now, in changing our understanding of the concept 'dimension,' we generate a widening host of parameters of description, which could readily include all our adjectives and adverbs, and even conjunctions and prepositions. I can go into a house, out of it, above or below it, through and beyond it, alongside and across it, with or without it, round and round and so on.

A related way to 'create' a construct is the continuum or spectrum, which is easy to share even with a child. The continuum is a scale or yardstick for a range of items to show how much each is more or less of something than the others; the critical bit is to recognize and name the something, which is some abstract quality. But start by placing them on a line stretching from the least to the most, or from one opposite to another. So, on a continuum called 'size,' an elephant is on the opposite end to the mouse, with a poodle dog in the middle somewhere.

You can make a scale between any two extremes; for instance between individual and group, immediate and long-term, volume and profit margin, home and work, realistic and ideal. As soon as you can name the yardstick that both embraces and distinguishes between all the items along its length, then you have abstracted an idea. It follows that you can pick any two factors significant to your problem, and by forcing them to become extremes to each other, you will derive some new construct.

We can then compare any number of 'similar' items, so long as we focus on the vital quality or concept we have recognized, and this comes from the concern you are facing. In water, we think of the length rather than height of a boat. When we choose 'height,' there must be no muddling it up with size, weight or importance, for we want giraffes or basketball players who are tall, not necessarily large or heavy! High jumpers and hurdlers need height, but what of pole-vaulters?

This may sound simple with a literal yardstick of length, measured in feet, but it can be applied to any collection of items all sharing some abstract property; they are similar in that the abstraction belongs to them all, but different according to their position on the scale. *Although the machine gun, grenade and flame-thrower are all multiple destroyers, they are not seen as Weapons of Mass Destruction (WMD) because they are so tangibly close to hand.* Actually one could construct a continuum of weapons according to their enormity:

Figure 13.3. a weaponry scale

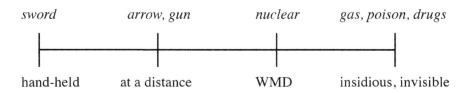

A child can place anything he meets on some continuum or other, even before he has recognized why it matters to put these items on the same yardstick. If he thinks of a razor blade, a pair of shears, a sickle, an axe, a wedge, and a stream, it may be easy enough to name the line or scale reflecting their relative strength. It's a quick way to show difference and similarity at once. What distinguishes this lot is clearly sharpness for cutting, with the stream at the blunt end. However, once there, it might remind you of how a friend ruined the paint on his back door by jet washing—just using too much pressure! Nowadays we use both water and air as cutting tools. You can see how this continuum idea connects the two quite different approaches to intelligence: reason and imagination.

In fact you could draw on any list of great painters and place them along a scale. Doing so would require you to name the scale in terms of which you were ordering them. It could be originality, beauty, conceptuality, execution, even value or relevance to today. On each scale, you might change their places, just as your friends, when asked to place them in order of merit, would vary their positions according to the scale or dimension or criterion they were adopting. Equally, by arbitrarily shuffling the order, you would produce further dimensions, perforce. It's a way of extruding additional concepts or ideas.

A new idea can be conceived even by stretching an existing continuum, as the microscope and telescope did from the Renaissance onwards. Nano technology might place the mouse pretty close to much larger animals; before nano-seconds, we counted in hours to years to centuries and once thought a person would disintegrate if they travelled faster than an ordinary motor-car, and more recently if they went through the 'sound barrier.' How does that compare with the latest telescope that measures cosmic rays at a shutter speed of a billionth of a second! There are more atoms in a grain of sand than there are grains of sand in the entire planet. It is even said by astro-physicists that our so-called universe may be only a small part of a great multi-verse of universes.

5. Cross-dimensions

A variation of this trick is to connect dimensions with one another and so create further dimensions. Thus alongside size comes length, thickness, density and so on until the image has sprouted outwards like this.

Figure 13.4. further dimensions

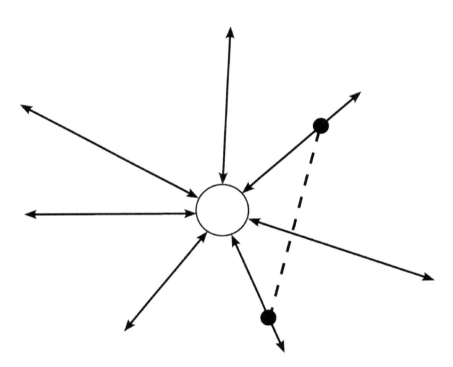

A new invention is often the result of applying a different technology to the subject's natural one, as in the multi-disciplinary approach embedded in Operational Research.

In what sense is a pound of feathers equal to a pound of pig iron? *What is the opposite to Napoleon?* Identifying an answer means having found some distinctive quality that may be hard to picture, but is real all right. Whilst a new idea can be conceived even by stretching an existing continuum, most often we just invent a new one to invite a new relationship. By forming connections sideways from one dimension to another, we can make a quantum leap in creativity.

- Linking 'weight' with 'color' on a transverse dimension is something we all employ for clothing and furnishings at home.
- Linking across our five senses is actually very common indeed, both physically or materially and metaphorically. To find the copper pipe or electric wiring buried behind plaster at home, we can 'see' it by tapping along the wall and listening for change of tone.
- Microsound is now a familiar technology to see the baby in the womb.
- In wine <u>tasting</u>, we use our nose. We also speak of using our 'nose' to assess the financial viability or risk of a project.
- We notice a brittle laugh, a hard look, a brown voice, a blue note in jazz, and the smell of tension in the room or the factory…

Seeing the potential is partly a matter of allowing it to come through the unconscious mind, which is a rich source of ideas that are not obvious and straightforward. Indeed there is no limit to the connections you can draw in your mind. Just ask your child to throw a bag of marbles onto a tray and count them. Say there were 24. Now, how many lines can she draw between them? We have seen that we can transform our 'memory' simply by making different connections or pathways between various items in it. *When the Table of Elements was formed, they thought each element was of itself pure: only later was it found that in different combinations they produce enormous variety.* Think chemistry. When someone puts together materials or ideas that had never been associated before, and achieves some excellent synergy between them as a result, we call it a breakthrough. Or when the ingenuity of the combination replaces the resources that had always been thought necessary. Pulling out a nail is easy with the leverage of a claw hammer.

A simple demonstration is to take a sheet of card, and write West on the extreme left edge and East on the extreme right. They are clearly as remote as can be in this context. Yet simply by including a third dimension, turning the sheet on one plane into a cylinder, it's shown how close they are. While this trick may be elementary, the principle is profound.

Some people when seeking an idea just go for some well-tried combination of thoughts. Others are keen enough to use more cross-references when searching their files, and keep their eyes open for longer. Thinking in holograms, like generating computer graphics with a light pen, makes it easier to see new contexts; thus paper can be made out of almost any material, a voice has color, music has texture, words can be bitter, and a landscape harsh. We can manufacture many such cross-contexts or planes of thought, simply by symbolic abstraction.

Just suspend any judgment during each flow of wild thinking. You need openness of mind and to give yourself permission to embrace the magical power of free association. Every aspect of your experience of life has formed connections which lead on in rapid succession, twisting and turning in all directions, acting like virtual synapses to send messages that might produce extraordinary notions. Encourage it. An early exponent of connectivism was Roget, whose scholarship produced his famous Thesaurus. Here is a sample of how a chain of notions works: *implication affinity essence gist pith scope synonym metaphor esoteric mystical symbolism allegory mystery arcane more than meets the eye deceptive secret suggestion clue glimpse inkling illumination light illustration simplification divination clairvoyance omen oracle presage insight empathy sympathy sensibility poetry transcendence incipience begin original out of reach dawns on you start fusion infusion suffusion join mix compound alloy unify make one.* Surely, no need for comment.

6. Reach for ideas

Indeed there is no limit to the images you can make and the connections you can draw in your mind. Such synergy does not merely add and subtract but has the greater conceptual power of multiplying or dividing. Putting 3 and 7 together might only add up to 10—or it could make 21. Galileo told us that "The book of the world is written in numbers," especially if you picture them spatially—or through force, weight, intensity, and so on.

Just as when you aim at a target or throw a ball, the actual trajectory simply disappears; the connection is usually more virtual than concrete and has to be envisioned. "We see the world not with our eyes, as it is, but with our brains, in a way that's useful to see." (David Carmel) No one has physical experience of the concepts of zero, of infinity, a black box or the square root of -1, but they have value. When trying to make a discovery, we know we don't really know, so we speculate, and in this book I suggest various ways to legitimize this and to show others what you are doing inside your mind and in whatever you say. I have found ways to invite and capture thoughts by adopting certain states of mind that stimulate you to reach new useful ideas, even on demand. Anyone can do this with practice: the trick is to place yourself somewhere else, and say or do things which will arouse faculties that you can't reach direct from within.

Suggesting some 'process' for thinking with imagination might be 'a red rag to a bull,' because the word smacks of a procedure, with a proper structure, order and sequence—anathema to the freedom you might desire. It takes the fun out of it, perhaps: maps and organized travel are OK for the tourist but not for the explorer, who wants to go where nobody has trod before, in his own way. I have much sympathy for this notion; perhaps you need a kind of random access to making at-first-irrational connections between images both inside and outside your experience. (Only later does the rationality appear, and that's when something exceptional actually does work.)

Any creative process will look 'mechanical' wherever it seems exceptionally clear and simple, but actually, a good process should be more organic than machine-like. *When your son first gets his new bicycle, it would take far longer to explain to him how to ride it and why really he won't fall off than for him to just get on and wobble away. Or ride it.* Somehow, the human body (and mind) both seem able to accomplish tasks of immense complexity, full of feedback and balancing systems, without quite knowing what's going on: consider how one can remain standing. Yet to become more expert, or to achieve anything exceptional, demands not only considerable analysis, but also bringing together all one's mental faculties, including passion and persistence. Dr. Alex Moulton's super-bike, with its tiny wheels, in 1986 created a world speed record of 51.29 mph. In 1958, his rubber suspension system helped Issigonis to design the mini, which could offer roominess in a tiny car. Both brought a new approach to design and are icons of engineering.

Excessively convergent analysis can suffer from 'paralysis by analysis,' from which the best escape is to think 'outside the box.' Categories that are utter strangers to one another can be brought together—and then you get a strange idea. Stars and wireworms are thought to be miles apart, yet in a few minutes, you can think up a very long list of similarities. *Is a red circle more similar to a green circle than to a red triangle?* Academically trained minds can find it hard to grapple with the notion of perceiving a short cut to almost impossible destinations, with the agility to actually take it. Is this fear or hubris? Anything new will cut across or violate some long-cherished value, belief or prediction, but ideas are born from <u>changing</u> the connections formed by experience.

How did that idea just come to me? When the classic light-bulb moment occurs, it may be either because you are searching for a solution and some idea 'rings a bell'; or that some incident or event pulled you to see its value, or a use for it. Are you happening to it or is it happening to you? This is why we are advised to incubate or 'sleep on it.' This cause–effect syndrome works both ways, as in *I love her, so she loves me—and vice versa*. Not only is this at the root of trading, it is why so much invention comes from working <u>together</u>.

A key part of innovation is to conceive a need for a product, what a 'market' would want and buy if it should ever get the chance. Clearly this is different from actually inventing the product, but it puts you ahead and in the right direction. I recall suggesting to a pharmaceutical client that they make it possible for a drug to be delivered directly to that part of the body needing it, and not throughout the system. Today, and only after many long years, this is almost achieved, though not yet perfectly. So, imagination leaps outside the person, beyond the objective world that surrounds him, up into a potential reality never yet experienced, and perhaps one that never will be. "To form an idea of a feeling is already to feel it in imagination"—you cannot help it, so Kant called it "the blind but indispensable function."

7. Vision

If you are considering some goal, and especially if you envision the even more strategic goal beyond it, a force-field of attraction is formed in its surrounding space so that questions hovering there resonate with the circling particles of idea and soon get sucked in. Why not encourage the flow or attraction on purpose, by raising questions consciously? At least learn to recognize an idea when others come up with them. The modern world needs to spend as much effort in connecting with ideas as protecting them, so nowadays companies are beginning to collaborate in research, rather than keep theirs secret.

Figure 13.5. Strategic vision (Cecil William Rhodes)

When you need to stretch out farther than you can actually see, you conjure an image out of thin air. The word 'envision' is bracketed with fantasy, but when proper judgment hasn't enough to go on, you make up for it. I don't mean 'being economical with the truth,' which of course no one would endorse: telling lies is clearly wrong, however you dress it up with modifiers and euphemisms. But vision is a neat way to describe the proper gift of imagination.

Departing from Jung's model, imagination is a form of thinking, sometimes the only vehicle available for thinking: it works to bring into mind a notion for which we have no experience in reality. We speak of 'conjuring up' ideas, but there really is no intent to deceive: you just believe in something out there which holds all the ideas no one has ever had yet. Let's pretend it is some kind of gassy atmosphere outside the globe of knowledge, a vessel mixing the familiar with the strange. What you get is an image not yet acquired: it can apply as much to an event in the past as in the future and also capture a quality you can perceive better than observe. Maybe after silicon, graphene? (This did earn Andre Geim and Konstantin Novoselov The Nobel Prize in Physics for 2010.) *So how about magnetic bacteria to build circuits, light instead of electricity, biology instead of physics*?

8. Unconscious mind

Imagination is characteristically flowing, so its information comes in more liquid form and lies fermenting in the unconscious, assuming infinitely changeable shapes and forces. It makes sense to use equally fluid, multi-dimensional ways of recognizing, retrieving and using it. Quality cannot always be measured by the quantities of the mechanistic paradigm: what you can count is often not what counts. A hologram in many dimensions comes to mind; based on waves, it offers more than a normal photograph, constructed of particles. So use the mind holistically, rather than by analysis, to allow one to find the real essence or spirit of reality that might not be found in its material parts. Where does life come from, and where does it go when you become dead?

Symbolic language is more powerful than its ordinary literal counterpart because it reaches into the unconscious pool of memory where profound feelings lie. Here is a rich source of images that are not obvious and straightforward. There's a gulf between what we observe and measure through our physical senses and what we feel only through our intuition; between feasible and potential. Only the obvious information we receive and hold comes in concrete form, specifically labeled and fitted into the right pigeonholes. To reach extra-ordinary ideas, go to the unconscious mind. It is reached by suggestion rather than by the explicit, direct enquiry or assault by reason; with subtlety, almost as if it needs to be wooed, like a reluctant maiden. Strangely, the unconscious is also the seat of decisiveness, the commitment to a course of action, rather than the sensible working through the logical connections between data.

Figure 13.6. Jodrell Bank radio telescope

Finally, I would like you to imagine yourself standing on the ground as if you were a radio telescope, a huge disk atop the mountains of Chile or at Jodrell Bank Centre for Astrophysics in Cheshire, UK, all the time scanning the universe. Of the billions of 'particles' received in your dish of life, one suddenly strikes the surface as an 'incident'—the simile is incident electrons. This thought-event means something that matters. The instant you make that divine connection, you have had an idea. *"Now three men in a railway carriage reading the paper are not a system—only when they engage in conversation do they become one"* (Professor F de P Hanika in New Thinking in Management). This explains how a face without beautiful features can be stunningly beautiful, due to how they all come together in a special, often asymmetric unity.

In reaching out with imagination beyond the limits of experience for a new idea, we do not really come from nowhere. Whilst perpetually scanning, we do have our own self within that radio telescope, and it has a significant effect on how likely we are to recognize an 'incident' at all, whether we perceive a use for it and complete the connection. Some people hardly ever 'get it' when a potential idea strikes their scanner; others do not feel justified in making any connection that is too unusual. We can even measure the likelihood for different kinds of people, through Rhodes' Thinking-Intentions Profile. But there is no one who simply cannot do so, and this book shows how anyone can improve the probabilities and so may offer hope to the downhearted!

Chapter 14

The Relevance Box

The Relevance Box is about how cause works and its role in coming up with exceptional ideas. Causality is silently working to explain how things happen, whether in the past or the future, even showing its impact on people, and vice versa. Reduction to bald Reason is objective and safe because it majors on things familiar and probable, based on how things normally happen. But what people feel subjectively may have even Stronger force because it harnesses effectiveness, why people will want to get the right thing actually done. And when the task is too challenging or aspiration exceptional, you need beyond all else to wonder beyond all else! Luckily ideas can come fast, so don't try it last. This chapter follows on from Your Strategic Approach in Chapter 3 and goes to the heart of thought. Everything we do is about the conjunction of Space and Time, the meaning we convey through the very structure of grammar, and the contribution of human feelings and perception.

This chapter brings you deep(er) into a core concept in thought: causality flows in every process from the rational logic of the Reductionist Box, through the Stronger Box of Feeling to the wild Box of Wonder beyond, lending some common structure even to the last. A major role for imagination is to think up unusual ways to <u>cause</u> or bring about what you want. So causality is the often-hidden factor in all that we achieve, all that happens to us and therefore all of our thinking, which includes imagination. It especially tells How things happen, but further Why people choose what to bring about and agree with, and how Else might things (be made to) happen. So brace yourself for a tough chapter which I have tried to make as simple as it allows.

Typically we ask,

> *What caused this? What does it cause? What might*
> *have caused it? What might cause this in future?*
> *What will it cause? What might it cause?*

Where you find any cause is at the collision of space and time. To hit a tennis ball, you time your swing to meet the space where the ball is: the result is the product of both. In grammar every sentence needs both a noun and a verb to make sense. In physics, matter IS and force DOES, so Einstein spoke of "matter and energy in space and time." These parameters act as two arms or vectors, the nouns representing identity and extending through space from close to remote; the verbs representing force and extending through time from obvious or probable to uncertain or unlikely. Both may stretch out infinitely, but you are more confident in making estimates when things are close rather than far off and obvious rather than uncertain.

1. The two parameters: how cause works

Please recognize that the next two illustrations work as graphs of two dimensions, on which you can take bearings, or plot the intersections of any approach.

Figure 14.1. The Reductive Box of Relevance

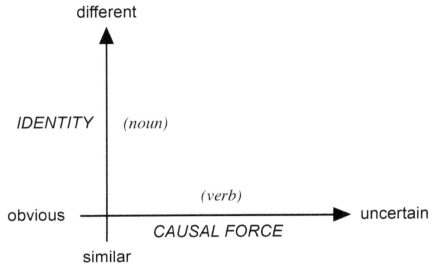

Figure 14.2. interlocking factors in space/time

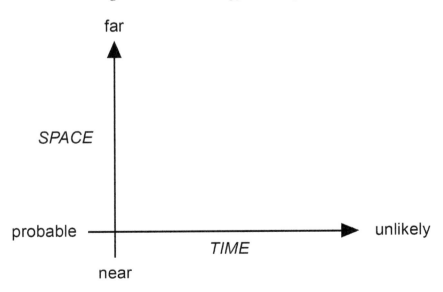

The vertical arm of identity reaches from similar to different, familiar to strange; the horizontal arm of time runs from obvious to uncertain, from now to change. Notice that the vertical stands for nouns or things, whilst the horizontal stands for verbs or causal force. Every sentence has to have both verb and (pro)noun to make any sense, as when 'This moves' or 'The rhinoceros charged him.' Both depend on differentiating and connecting, and also about space and time, so they join up grammar and science in an essential common meeting-ground.

The vertical arm in space reaches from near to far, and also explicit and clear to implicit and cloudy. The horizontal arm of time runs from probable to unlikely and both parameters run from immediate to remote in both space and time. Specifically, space is about direction, and motion works through time. So to find your position at sea, you must know how far north you are for the angle of the sun in space; but also you need a chronometer to reflect time.

Modeling like this is a simple way to explain 'co-incidence,' or cause, but because it is so profound, it's hard for some people to take in at first. However, to go further with this construct is really worthwhile.

The time parameter shows 'how likely is **a** to cause **b**' and 'because **a** therefore **b**'; and a prediction such as 'if **x** then **y**.' The space parameter concerns how 'alike' particular things are, what are their attributes and characteristics; this means if something happens to one thing it is likely also to affect another, similar, thing. *When a virus strikes, the cause of illness is not just the virus, otherwise everyone present would suffer: it is its interaction with something distinguishing the people who are struck down.* A wrong diagnosis assures a wrong prescription. Further, every plan or product that doesn't work will have missed some causal combination of ingredient and action. When designing anything new, we must ask 'Exactly what change in what thing has to be made to bring about the result desired?' Medical cures are hard to discover because they at first cannot get the right action to coincide with the right thing. They may almost go for hitting a six but get caught on the boundary! It demands the discipline of making connections that have been previously ignored because they are highly improbable, dissimilar and remote. So risky.

Cause informs not only the choice of the best option, but also the testing of your evaluation, so causality suggests scenarios of what might go wrong, but also how you could prevent it and how to cushion the consequences in advance. Whenever we forget this, we design things that don't work, we fail to anticipate whatever might spoil our well-laid plans, take the wrong actions to correct poor performance, suffer costs that were almost entirely needless waste, envision hopeless strategies, fail to learn from our mistakes, or to persuade people to adopt what we think is best.

2. The Stronger Box of Feelings

In Chapter 3, the three levels of Strategic Approach were explained as if they were aspects of a 'Relevance Box.' The Reductive Box of Relevance showed how an action we are taking will work (or not!) but not why we want to take it, the field of the Stronger Box outside it. The former declares, "It will cause what happens (according to laws)," e.g. code breaker, physics/math, the inevitable outcome governed by how the world operates. The latter says, "I will cause what I want to happen (according to my will/conscience)," e.g. murderer, intention, hope, the human, subjective reasons for bringing it about. What does it all mean? The trouble is, language has become so loose that people often say why when they mean how, just as they may say when to mean where: Q. How far is the nearest pub? A. About 5 minutes. It is certainly worth being clear about these two differing halves of causality.

I recall a science fiction radio play in which mankind had been wiped out from the planet, and most of the play was about its various terrifying consequences. Yet the question to raise was "Why did any of these outcomes matter any more?" for things are important only because of the people they affect. What we personally experience or feel we can handle is full of bias, values, predictions and fears that overcome rational thought. *In an Olympic track event, the outside lane offers a gentler curve and is logically the best lane—but in the inner lane you can see your competitors from behind, so they pull your motivation along.* Moreover, a good orator can sway an audience by the way he puts his message across, so that in a crowded square, even people of sound mind would join in 'Heil Hitler' and follow him to hell.

Figure 14.3. The Stronger Box of Relevance

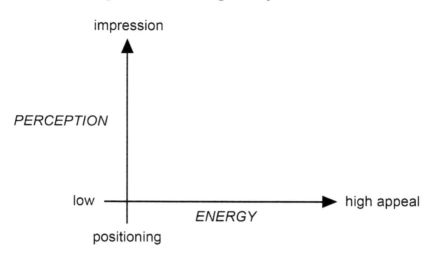

The vertical arm of our box is about position in space and personal view-ing-point or perception. Each person is influenced by the extent they observe through all their senses and how they reflect this through the lens of their experience. Where do we position our encounter, in the scale of things: are we seeing the full picture but not the detail, what's the scope of our horizon for it? The 'message' or image we receive may well be affected by the way it comes to us, the impression we form of it. Feelings can easily see ugly and beautiful as similar, when necessary. Your 'Warm' mode means strong, reso-lute, intense in quality, effective, fast and forceful, subjective and personal; it does not mean weak, but rather has the strength of being flexible, like steel wire. Looking at your own body, it is easy to feel that your bones must be stronger than your tissue, because they need to be rigid, else their function as levers would not work. Yet your more flexible sinews will stand up to nine tons, just as wood can be a 'stronger' building material than iron.

In the Stronger Box, the horizontal arm of causality reflects warm human energy. The sacrifices made to achieve a high goal strongly held achieve the apparently impossible. *To rescue her child, a mother has been known to seize the bumper and lift up the whole weight of the car.* People climb Everest without oxygen and walk to the Poles unaided. Look what paraplegics have achieved in their Olympics.

I find this extremely moving, personally. As a young man I took athletics seriously, being fortunate to be up at Oxford together with Chris Chataway, Derek Johnson and both the Pinningtons, among several Olympic medal-winners. I trained regularly with them as a member of the University Athletics Club and was there to witness the famous four-minute mile of Roger Bannister, who came before me to be President of Exeter College Athletic Club. Bob Shaw, another medalist, was elected President just after me, and is a life-long friend. I continued my interest, and in the school where I became a master I developed athletics into a major part of school life, so we could take on schools many times our size. I coached Michael Parry to win the half-mile in the 1956 All-England Schools Championships in record-breaking time; in doing so he was then the fastest schoolboy in the world recorded at this distance.

Then I suffered polio and my life changed. I joined the commercial world without full use of my limbs and for forty years have had to use up a lot of energy to get back on par. All this is simply to show at first hand how rational probability is everywhere overturned by the human factor. *If the honey is on a branch that is too slender, even the hungry bear will not go there—but a person might.*

When it comes to immediacy for action, the subjective may feel more concrete and apparent than the objective kind, which is more abstract and less tangible. So it takes priority. As confidence in your judgment begins to wane or falter, it's a signal to go for richer information than mere reasoning has demanded. An equation or a formula has tremendous potential because it works on everything it represents, and will do so for all time and for everyone. The sublime potential of an oil painting by Titian, a symphony by Beethoven or a sonnet by Shakespeare lies in their provoking in different ways an enormous range of insights.

These principles apply also to the influence of feelings and emotions, which explain Why people want or like something. Human energy is so powerful and so personal that it can either assure greater success or destroy your project. This is what you really FEEL, and why this is called The Stronger Box.

Logically, in the 'Cool' physical world, cause must always come before its effects: the lightning must have struck the tree before it withered. With human beings it is different: they can think up what effects they hope for, and then imagine what might cause them. They make 'wrong' things work by forcing them to conform; for instance if you really are up the creek without a paddle, then any old plank is made to become one. The Stronger Box allows passion even when we really know that it won't work. *Escaping the Titanic, you grab a framed photograph rather than a bottle of water or a woolly hat, because you love her.* What is <u>required</u> for survival may not be so <u>desired</u> as the more spiritual 'feeling.' This is why hope easily rules prediction and you turn a blind eye to inconvenient facts and common sense when you have made up your mind to act. Ironically, even academic or scientific disciplines succumb to this when taking more notice of <u>who</u> someone is than <u>what</u> they actually say.

3. Wonder beyond...

Imagineers look more towards the Improbable and the Remote ends of those Relevance parameters. What only <u>seems</u> similar or different, immediate or remote? Perhaps an unusual stance might surprise us with an unlikely course of action. To begin with the horizontal vector of probability, suppose we pretended that the most likely approach to a problem would fail; if we then go for the most unlikely solution, is this really so daft? Are we not constantly taken aback by how events really unfold? In war or contest, surprise can be one's most decisive weapon.

Figure 14.4. The Relevance Box: I wonder beyond

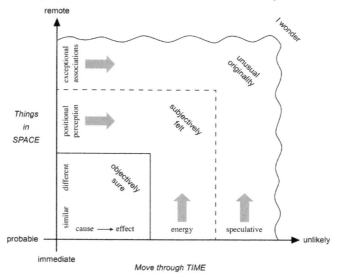

Here we are outside the box, or in the box outside. It reminds us how cause works: we move things to achieve any result. So when we seek exceptional originality, we look for things that are other or else that we can connect; and what we value and commit to will be unlikely and probably astonishing.

On the vertical parameter, suppose we purposely shifted our perception of the key thing in our problem. We could alter our view of it, look for different attributes and characteristics, or treat it as remote or distant rather than close or immediate. Well, what then? Seeking a cure for cancer or diabetes is seen as more purposeful and worthy than finding out how cells work; coming up with a computer driven by light is more remote than improving the electronics on existing computers. So innovation that is constricted by obvious and immediate needs will probably win its budgets. However, it will be ignoring huge opportunity, which, if someone else finds it first, might even destroy the company. This is part of the issue about investment to enable non-astronauts to travel into space. Sir Martin Rees, when Astronomer Royal and President of The Royal Society, said firmly that "Our best work is unpredictable," and this is at the crux of why we must go beyond logic, feelings and even common sense.

Else is extra-ordinary: an extra dimension of thought massively expands both complexity and possibilities, as when 6 squared = 36, but 6 cubed is 216. To seek the spirit of otherness is slightly off-center, so those who do so often are seen as literal 'eccentrics,' people who are foreign, strange or alien! Imagineers are outsiders, their talents both despised and adored.

Much thinking is about trying to bring closer together what is and what should be. The infinite space outside is to conceive what might be, what might happen if we were to do whatever we might. This is to pretend things could go a different way altogether. Another side of Else is *If*. A whole chapter (12) is devoted to it. What else might happen if…? If it were done this way, if we were to pursue that vision, then what might be brought about?

Now we seek ideas as different and as far out from the usual as we can, at the extremes of those parameters. Seek the outrageous and the challenging, the improbable and irrelevant. Abandon what is known to cause things and what is feasible, in favour of change and originality. Even find that which at first sight violates criteria—so long as you keep the goal firmly in mind.

Crucially, it means to try the shock and awe of surprise, to go from familiar to strange. This is psychologically a huge stride which entails a change of mindset from critical thinking and emotional values. It offers not only permission to play the wild card, but also limitless scope for any and all kinds of imagination. In another analogy, if we treat the Reductive Box as solid structure, and the Stronger Box as liquid hydraulic power, then Wonder is like a ballooning gas.

In writing this very book, I have become aware that WHY was the focus of my first book, *The Colours of Your Mind*, written with my wife. My second book, *Conceptual Toolmaking*, was about HOW things get done. The present book explores further the ELSE. This could explain how *The Colours* had high appeal to Feelers of the Stronger Box, and *Conceptual Toolmaking* to Reasoners, those denizens of the Reductive Box. If so, I hope *I Wonder* will reveal how Imagineering works, while catching the connections and relevance for the other two components of the trinity.

Figure 14.5. Modeling How, Why, Else

How things work

What **else** to explore?

Why things matter

As soon as you face an impossibility, or when you aspire to the outstanding, you enter the world of Else. In this domain you blot out sensible rules so as to expand the horizons. There really are, as Hamlet said, "more things in heaven and earth, Horatio, than are dreamt of in your philosophy." It is said that Man has learned more science in living memory than in the whole history of civilization. I suspect that future generations may have to unlearn much of our present 'knowledge' and discover many times more. Now you can connect things that are extremely different or unlikely. Only a fool will keep on with the same action, hoping for a different outcome. *When a rock fails to split from your hardest hammer blows, you strike it somewhere else, and then it miraculously falls apart.*

To generate new ideas, either escape from the vice-like grip of hard information, so necessary for the analytic Reasoner, or exploit it by pushing exceptionally hard. Accuracy and precision can act as a discipline which offers either ingenious possibilities or no scope at all. As every engineer knows, it is often desirable to go for a loose fit rather than a tight one. Even John Harrison, the brilliant maker of the marine chronometer that made accurate navigation possible for the first time (in the 18th century), at first fell into this quality trap. Though he was working in wood, not metal, he was so exacting as to make the meshing of the teeth too 'perfect,' so that the movement actually failed to move! We need to give ourselves permission to be loose, rough and even vague—but, crucially, on purpose!

This goes beyond the art of approximation and the willingness to do it, which represent a critical skill and attitude of a manager. A new idea is not to be guaranteed by aiming for any specific direction <u>towards</u> it, because being new, nobody knows where the 'it' is. What can be done is to go <u>away from</u> what is known, in some direction not already pursued; it's like convergence and divergence in thought. A goal or target demands convergence on it, whilst to explore cannot, else it would not be an exploration. Know whether to push out from your inside or pull in from outside.

Failure to venture outside the norm is unlikely to produce any outstanding idea(s). Yet oddly enough it is sometimes the <u>smallest</u>, most nuanced change that will do just the trick—so long as it's unorthodox. For those who are not naturally Imagineers, reaching farther than one can see demands huge energy, courage and skill to overcome caution and conformity. One almost needs permission to risk going too far out along your special cantilever. Clearly, this can be dangerous: you pay a penalty for being the only one in step or for finding a challenging way forward. The apparent madness entailed in Wonder might frighten the horses stuck with their feet in the ground, but imagination lifts you out of the rut, to fly higher than mere feelings, and above all to reach unusual heights fast. Through wonder, you create a special kind of 'information' before you deserve it.

Anything less obvious has to be imagined. Finding cause in the past has the advantage that it has already happened, so there are facts to be found and brought together: finding how to cause what you want to happen is therefore harder—but the same causal principles apply to diagnosing the future as to diagnosing the past. The key is the precision, accuracy, detail and completeness of your data, identifying what is or has to be special, and finding the relationships between them.

But these three realms of Relevance don't have to be tackled in any one order: in fact, wisdom demands you move between them, sometimes even beginning with Wonder. Be clear, only the trivial or routine can be handled without it. The extra-ordinary needs you to go forward and upward in seeking ideas, backward in assessing their value, and sideways to assure the fuel and support of Feelings.

"The world is perishing for lack of wonder."
G K CHESTERTON

Chapter 15
Is Wonder Spiritual?

To wonder is a fluid, wide open questioning, whereby we seek the spirit of some new truth and use imagery to bridge to a more tangible answer. Thinking itself is more abstract than concrete or material, and you wonder about something that cannot yet exist in your mind, so even more sublime. Imagination "spirits something out of the air", just as the invisible soul of an idea is captured by art. It can tune in with magical resonance to produce astonishing effect. The energy of wonder transcends ordinary motivation, producing the flash of immediacy and inspiration. All this gives us a sense of the divine.

Wonder is so slippery, abstract and intangible that it's hard to discuss making things up without concepts such as 'virtual reality' and 'spiritual.' Some people may react to the latter by reaching for their revolver, but no need to assume it means 'holy' unless in the archaic sense of wholeness, borrowed by Jan Smuts when he coined the word 'holistic.' You can think of spiritual as non-material, more like gas than liquid or solid, especially as it can appear or disappear in an instant and may be hard to get hold of. This kind of thought is as elusive as quicksilver, but picturing is ideal for capturing concepts, trading or building with them and storing in memory.

"Myth does not mean something untrue,
but a concentration of truth."
DORIS LESSING, AUTHOR

The exact letter of the law or an agreement is notorious for not being the equal of its spirit that flows between the other elements, either to lubricate their interaction or to glue them all together. It is spiritous energy, or a special form of motivation, that connects wonder with emotion. And even naming is a kind of insight that that sees resemblance between various things, some closeness in time or space, some causal relationship. The very conceiving of the need for some new solution <u>before anyone wants it</u> is an act of genius.

Thinking is actually a spatial activity, needing a vehicle to capture what's going on between our motor system, our organic chemistry and our electrical nervous system. We can usually see information and its sources, and we can always be sure to come to judgment, even though it might be wrong. But conjuring up a new idea out of nothing— one that will transcend the difficulties that face me, or bring a vision of impossible wonder—that's a different kettle of fish.

Imagination may be outside science for some people, but it is an essential input and driver of new knowledge that enables us to see what is not really there (yet). We have seen that many ideas are born from making connections and disconnections between what is already in your experience: this relationship seems intangible and spiritual. To create a bridge between the virtual experience inside the mind and what is material and real in the world outside, we use imagery as a kind of language for the very processes of thought, especially those that operate under rules very different from normal critical thinking.

"In my mind's eye, Horatio."
WILLIAM SHAKESPEARE, *HAMLET*

If material matter is dead unless it has something spiritual moving within it, are life forces 'spirit'? In Latin, the word *spiritus* means breath (of life or *animus*), and Ovid wrote "to be living or alive means to change constantly." Life goes out of any living thing, like a flower, an animal and even a human being, when their thrusting spirit wanes.

The life of an idea comes from two inner sources: emotion and the spirit. These are not always working together, but once they do, your thought takes on unbeatable force. The excitement that takes you over and enflames you with a sort of passion to believe in it and bring it about can be either <u>for</u> something new and desirable or <u>against</u> something feared or disliked. I think passion is mostly seen as the force of emotion and human motivation, but I wonder if when focused on something new, more than good, it is the spirit of imagination. For me this is still a kind of mystery, which so many philosophers have struggled with.

There is certainly something of the mystical, magical or visionary, bringing a sense of huge power in the moment. Imagination and the spirit surely have this ineffable quality in common, that both of them simplify and unify, trying to find uniting principles, and this is like forming an idea. Both are apt to go ahead of the information available—or do without it!—both can be rough and ready and not precise, and they both bring to bear great energy. If you are under torture, your tormentors might try to change your mind; they can certainly affect what you know, and even what you believe in. What they cannot attempt is to alter what you can imagine, for this is so deep within your heroic spirit as to be unreachable by anyone but you—and even for you that's hard enough!

1. Thinking itself is spiritual
Thinking is to be treated with awe, perhaps a force field entirely beyond our ken, which occasionally finds a resonance with our inner being. Naturally, any

kind of thinking is 'spiritual' as distinct from material. But as soon as you look for something new, it must by definition be different from what you already know and also what you believe to be right, since if it were the same, it would not be new. Of course, you hope your new insight might prove to be both true and good, but this cannot be guaranteed <u>before</u> you have reached it.

"Where on earth is Heaven?" (Jonathan Stedall, a question from his young son.)

My case is supported by the evolution of intelligence, as witnessed and traced in "A History of the World" presented through the BBC by the British Museum in 2010. *The Director, Neil McGregor, selected just 100 objects from the millions in its collection. The artifacts chosen go from the stone chopper found in the Rift Valley and dated to 1,800,000 years ago, which was the rational and practical solution to the need to kill, skin and cut up wild animals.* Over the centuries, Man developed from this crude hand tool, which itself put real demands for thought on its maker. In this journey, he progressed from practical utility to copying and re-presenting the reality found in nature, such as the male and female reindeer carved on an elephant tusk 16,000 years BC and found in France. Later still, he began to go from the reality he could see and touch towards whatever he might conceive beyond that, adding more and more refining objectives and skills, with an element of art in both his product and his mind. It is on this more 'virtual' level that I believe his imagination reached out for and blended with some kind of spirituality. If this be even roughly true, it could help justify my claim that Imagination should be respected, not just as equal with Truth and Judgment but even, perhaps, above. Wordsworth wrote of

"…imagination, which in truth
Is but another name for absolute power
And clearest insight, amplitude of mind,
And Reason in her most exalted mood"

- Nearly all our 'knowledge' comes actually from using our imagination, for most of the time we have not 'experienced' it directly, only in images. For instance what we 'know of' a Siberian temperature of minus eighty degrees Celsius, a vast iron ore mine in the Australian desert, and most of what we have read in books or from talk of others,

216

has been received second-hand. So often the play we have heard on the radio lives on in pictures far more vivid than if we had seen it on television or film. Homo sapiens, wise or thinking Man, seems to require very little information so as to form the whole picture, which he does by discerning invisible connections. I remember the first time I was shown (in the 1960s by IBM) a film of a person in total darkness walking towards us, conveyed simply by lights placed on just a few places on the body. We could see the pattern of movement, which alone told us it was a person moving. So few dots, so much meaning!

- In a graph, we complete the curve as if we can see real points making a continuous line between the points.
- Moving film captures x events per second, which we then string together in our mind as if those pictures are moving, so that we can study not only the way the legs of a horse actually move but also how a crocus opens in the Spring.
- When we multiply numbers together, say 8 and 17, instead of adding up 17 eight times, we make an amazing swoop to 136: just think of the work saved with much larger numbers.
- The Romans could survey and build straight roads over huge distances: using Vs, Xs, Ls, Cs and Ms; when I was little, I wondered, how ever did they manage all their multiplications before Arabic numerals? (Of course they had to find a way to simplify and they chose halving and doubling.)

In 2009 a Nigerian terrorist succeeded in boarding a trans-Atlantic plane with explosives attached to his thighs, aiming to kill all the passengers in dying for his 'cause.' It seems that the CIA had all the data required to identify him in advance, but as President Obama declared, they just '*failed to join up the dots*' between the data, and turn it into information. Extending this to a more conceptual field, whenever the dots are too few, when the spaces between them stretch too far for extrapolation, then the only way to make the connection or bring the insight is by imagination.

2. Capture the spirit of truth

Imagination captures the 'spirit,' which is more of the reality than what we see with our eyes. We find it too in music, as with John Tavener. It is this form of image that the poet sees and tries to express: the core or kernel of the matter. The concept of 'image' when applied to a corporation, institution or even a government or political party is just the same. It works also for your own personal strategy for life—who you really are and what's the career and contribution to the world that would best suit you. Forget the deviations of some low quality Public Relations consultants, who attempt to paint a gloss on what the company is really like, so as to appeal to the market and other stakeholders. *Wally Olins, in his book* The Corporate Personality *(1978), makes it very clear how crucial it is to delve down and find the reality of the organization, the authentic nature of the business and its strategy, what it is really like and is trying to bring to the world.* Capturing this spirit and then expressing it is work of a high order. Get it wrong or fail to convey how it strategically influences everything done by and within that organization, and the business will fail to live up to its promise. It is because many of the world's banks have so lost sight of their real or original purpose that we had the banking crisis of the Noughties. This is approaching what Kant and Schopenhauer called the 'noumenal' as distinct from the phenomenological aspect of reality or truth.

"A picture is worth a thousand words," just as the word is worth a thousand pictures, because all our words are actually metaphors, some more or less obvious images than others. They can be as redolent of meaning as the equation is of number, or a formula as law. It is such patterns by which we remember, make sense of, interpret significance of, and take short cuts with. We even use this giant concept to determine day-to-day things, such as whether to make a bolt or a nut, or to use a hexagonal Allen key from inside the bolt or a spanner from outside the hexagonal nut. Abstractions might not feel 'spiritual' but the thought entailed certainly is. As William Blake remarked, "All events in nature have a spiritual cause."

3. Insight

Reaching conclusions, indeed thought of all kinds, is the result of abstract processes, virtual action inside the mind. As long as we keep thoughts inside, there is no pressure to commit to them, so we are safe until we turn them into real action in the world outside, perhaps by telling someone else. As soon as we 'name' something for the first time, we have had to form some kind of image in order to capture its characteristics. We seek the *Distinction*, a kind of pattern, which although not in itself visible is discernible nonetheless. We use these pictures, however unconsciously, to make comparisons between similar things to see how they are different, and how even different things are similar, and altogether to guide our lives.

The art of naming feels like a divine insight, yet you do it each time you name a file on your computer—only to find out later you got it wrong and cannot find it! It should clarify the rough impression, making it easier to remember and use. It is this joining together of a concrete sense-experience and an abstract intellectual construct that marks what Kant called 'transcendental association' or active imagination. He makes a nice contrast between the images formed in the mind of five objects arranged on the table and the Arabic/Indian numeral 5.

Figure 15.1. a pentagon versus the numeral?

Centuries ago, people wishing to memorize anything long or complex would position each 'idea' in a certain place, say within a known building, so that later on, by scanning the building in their mind they would be reminded of every item. They could thus perform prodigious feats of memory (Frances Yates, *The Art of Memory*). This spatial positioning works equally well for sketching out our thoughts, perhaps on Post Its, to assemble into the most meaningful pattern or map. A new idea, the nub of it, is a coming together of various images not defined or quantifiable, but suddenly their spirit is recognized. What are the first impressions we form on the instant we meet someone—and which tend to persist for a long time? *What is it that we fall in love with, if at first sight?* It is this which may be all that remains when stored in the memory, and in some battered photograph in your wallet or handbag. No one else will ever be quite like him or her.

The soul or signature

We speak of the soul, not only of a person but also to capture some essence of life, joining non-material thought inside the mind with more physical action in the world outside. The aim of intuition is to reveal an insight into realities that had <u>not</u> before been experienced. What is special about an individual person is expressed in a painter's portrait, more powerfully than merely their facial features. *Likewise, the architect tries for resonance between the building and the spirit of place.* Ravel actually managed to convey the spirit of Spain in his "Bolero," without ever having been there. It is surely this characteristic that makes people equate 'art' with creative imagination. Equally, a law of physics cannot be seen or touched, yet it is there to be recognized.

> *"Consciousness is spiritual, not part of the physical world of science. It is subjective, whereas science is objective… Consciousness creates an observer-independent reality."*
> JOHN SEARLE IN TED TALKS 23 JULY 2013

This is why it is hard to capture someone's intention. Just as the eye itself is an extension of the brain, so imagination "spirits something out of the air" in a common phrase. Works of art, whether paintings, sculptures, music, dance or poetry, also hold within them this 'signature' of their maker. Just to recognize the person telephoning you through one word (only) entails massive complexity of analysis, yet we speak her name instantly.

Similarly, turning on the radio, only a very few notes enable you to recognize the composer, even if you have never heard the piece.

- Whenever you're not quite sure whether it be Mozart or Haydn, Purcell or Byrd, Dvořák or Tchaikovsky, it is because the spirit of the composer has not been felt by you; no question whether the Beatles or the Rolling Stones, of course!
- When men like van Meegeren fake a great master, they are successful insofar as they have been able to capture, for example, Vermeer, the

way he painted, not just what the picture looks like: more the verb than the noun.

- W Graham Robertson (1866–1948), the artist, who collected William Blake and then gave the collection to the nation, was once asked why he had never made a self-portrait. "Because I am not my style" was his reply.

When we notice someone's 'style' it may be this 'quality' that eludes accurate and material description—for it is something of the spirit that we are seeking to describe. *Portia was able to win, to overcome the exacting demands of Shylock*: compassion and real truth over-rules. When it is unable to put this wisdom into practice, "the law is a ass," as A P Herbert so pungently declared.

There are of course nouns that are concrete and others known as abstract. Yet in even the most concrete things, there is an abstract quality, one that cannot be specified but which is very much there. We speak of its characteristic, its very 'nature.'

4. Energy amazes

Perhaps the 'spiritual' nature of an idea or of wonder is comparable to motive force on a higher level. The esprit of a regiment is such a nebulous kind of image, yet often far stronger than the number of troops and guns left at the end of a battle. In the Congo, it is said that sorcerers "eat the spirit" of people. And Cesar Millan, the Mexican-American 'dog whisperer,' speaks of "using more of my spiritual than my psychological energy." When you go to the races, and view horses like Red Rum or Frankel parading in the ring before the race, just observe the horse you are thinking of backing: see and feel his spirit, because if you cannot, you should find another horse to put your money on!

Just as *Heineken gets to those parts other beers cannot reach* so wonder seems to penetrate and uplift, like brandy, our other faculties of mind. Any picture of the future which is a quantum leap beyond what we are used to feels like inspiration: literally we draw in our <u>breath</u>. A sense of the heroic brings a rush of blood to the heart, a lump in the throat or tears to the eye. Could you ever forget the 'War horse' of that stage play by Michael Morpurgo?

I do know at first hand that some exceptional inventors are very wary of a researcher's effort to discover from them the secret of how they are so brilliant and prolific in coming up with outstanding inventions. You get the sense that they feel their gift is sacred and fragile and might disappear if investigated too closely. Like love, it is too special to be made public. And these are scientists! Perhaps they secretly cherish flair, and hope that some of the magic, the intuition of genius, will remain intangibly elusive, out of reach of others' understanding or research. The quality of our ideas will always be more effective than mere brute force: it is how we outwit the machine age we have made, lest it become our master.

5. Spirituality is to do with relationship

As said in the previous chapter, ideas are born from making connections and disconnections between things, to form a new image. The spiritual nature of imagination is then to do with relationship: the force in the space <u>between</u> images or events, rather like magnetic force or gravity, chemistry or hydraulic pressure, which you cannot actually see. Intuition has a 'virtual' connotation, recognized by Spinoza as another and yet higher level of knowledge: "the immediate insight into truth that comes when we grasp a proposition and its proof in a single act of mental attention" (Roger Scruton). Such images are seen as outside and beyond 'normal thought,' and yet they lie at the very heart of our being. Revealing these mysterious virtual processes as mental tools, so that you can see which ones to use for any situation you face, is the work of my 'thinking-intentions,' for they reflect the <u>spirit</u> of your thinking.

> *"When a wise man points at the stars,*
> *only a fool stares at his finger."*
> CONFUCIUS

Over the centuries we have developed the wonderful properties of mathematics, in which even the elementary functions of multiply, zero, infinity, algebraic formulae and the earliest geometry turn out to be profound and powerful in the imagery they make possible. Imagination is like this: tremendously effective without having any apparent substance, weightless, airy, if not shapeless. A concept rather than a picture, an abstract formation in the mind rather than anything concrete. We have grown our scientific understanding of 'invisible' forces such as electricity, chemical reaction, gravity, centrifugal and heat expansion, nutrients, nano-technology, radio, X-rays, infrared and wireless communication: the list is endless. We have discovered the magical properties of the mirror and the spiral, and how blood is more than a 'thing,' it's a force of life. Life itself is still a mystery—so scientists find that however many lifeless elements they put together they are still unable to bring any life to them that they did not already possess, as in chemicals.

So when discussing idea inspiration, it is quite hard to avoid the elusive quality that faith and intuition share, in going beyond what can be known: we believe something is true, or has happened, or will happen or means something; just as we feel inspiration for an idea, without hard facts or evidence, as when "It gave me just the glimmer of a thought" (Spirax Sarco director). An idea is instinctive, a kind of 'spiritual emotion' like belief, in that you cannot guarantee to earn an idea, but rather it's a gift of 'grace.'

Inspiration, faith and intuition share the elusive quality of going beyond or ahead of what can be known. Those of us who are unusually inventive rarely feel that we have really 'created' anything absolutely on our own, but rather that we seem to sense some kind of resonance with whatever surrounds us, so that it becomes an insight. It's only analogy, but we know from physics that a really high soprano can shatter a glass, that a vehicle can break if driven at a speed which coincides with the undulations of a road in mining country—I know, since it happened to my Autosleeper over mining country in Belgium! Never mind the particles, where is this mysterious frequency? How can we learn to catch the wave, as we do when riding the surf?

I quote here a paragraph from the memoirs published by Rolls-Royce of a friend and neighbor, Dr. Alex Moulton, whose name will always live on in his astonishing new concept for the bicycle. I also met Dr. Noboru Tominari, a key person in its adoption by the Japanese tire company, Bridgestone. In his autobiography, Alex said, "From Dr. Tominari I learnt the Japanese practice of 'detecting the spirit' of an artefact which is made… It works in this way I believe: when an artefact is made, either by a great deal of loving care by one artisan, such as the Samurai sword maker, or by the multiple work of many people working under the leadership of one man, they say it has acquired the 'spirit' of its creator. *By seeing or using the artefact one can detect its spirit*. I was delighted to find that on the Bridgestone Moulton they wrote (nothing to do with me at all) the words 'The Spirit of Bradford-on-Avon', by which I was deeply honoured."

Design is too often seen merely as the aesthetic icing on the cake whereas it is really the essence of the cake itself, producing its quality, efficiency, effectiveness and appeal. *Asked whether Concorde was designed to be beautiful, an engineer concerned replied,* "Oh no, our wind-tunnel showed us that this was simply the best shape to go so fast" (Victoria & Albert Museum exhibition on British design, July 2012). What divine synergy. It has a special appeal to me because I live in the ancient Gloucestershire town of Wotton-Under-Edge, from where came leaders in the development of both Concorde and its Olympus Rolls-Royce engine.

Figure 15.2. the beauty of Concorde

When things and people work together exceptionally well, it is well called 'chemistry,' because it seems like magic or alchemy. Choosing the right color of paint costs not a penny more than any other, but makes the whole room wonderful instead of bland, ordinary or horrid! And ballast in a sailing boat might feel like pigs of iron, yet where you place it affects steering, stability and safety, and speed. Quality is like that too.

You often cannot count what counts and it is the least tangible aspects of life and thought that command the greatest significance, especially those you don't yet know about. Just as the laws of sub-atomic physics work differently from those governing the material world we normally experience, so the laws of spirituality might play the same tricks, and even share them with the universe of imagination. I have as much duty to think Else about the world as to think beyond myself to consider others. I believe it is immoral not to think as well as you can, and this entails that you orchestrate <u>all</u> your faculties, especially one you cannot readily grasp.

When a scientist, an engineer, a mathematician tries to express the spiritual quality of something encountered, he comes up with 'beauty.'

V
So What?

Chapter 16
So What?

In these days of almost chaotic change, every person and every business is into innovation, else they be left behind. Yet too few realise that Innovation divides sharply into two quite different tasks: inventing new concepts, ideas, products and ways of living; versus winning acceptance for the idea and bringing it into action: innovation with a small i. The gulf between these two is so daunting and unrecognised that most ideas suffer shipwreck. The two roles differ and usually require differing kinds of person.

Here I have tried to show how coming up with unusual ideas on demand requires a special thinking approach, but there is a wide range of options to choose from if you glimpse how it could change your life – or those of your nearest and dearest. We really can model thought so as to become more aware of how we are thinking, using a common language for sharing our intentions.

Sound theory, built from years of experience, may well open up your mind, but is no use until you do something with it. Every little success will encourage you to learn for yourself, more and more. If this book has given any inspiration, do act on it or email jdr@thunks.com and personal development at http://effectiveintelligence.com/more.

1. The gulf between invention and innovation

Wonder is not much use until you do something about it: a bright idea butters no parsnips until you move from its invention to innovation: winning support, acceptance and usage. I confess that for too many of my ideas I have failed to follow through, else I would be very rich indeed! Actually, the originator of an idea is often the worst person to secure its innovation, because having stretched out wide to close on an unusual solution, he cannot see why others don't grasp the connection he has made. The gap opened up that challenges received wisdom needs bridges of communication and persuasion. It needs time, effort of a different kind of thought, perhaps different people.

2. The role of inventors

Initiatives arise out of conceiving a need for something that may not be wanted yet, as well as coming up with how to deliver it or its solution. Inventing what everyone wants is tempting, but spotting the need first reduces competitors and also makes more dramatic progress. Sometimes the solution comes before the need, as in the laser.

The lone inventor becomes more rare as knowledge multiplies daily and globally. Who brings what to the table matters more and more, though the individual still needs his islands of quiet space on his own. Inventors are excessively eager to learn; for them the strange is more fun than the familiar, so they require a lot of tolerance from everyone else. Their mind-set is probably different, except that even they succumb to feelings when opposition is too severe. They usually have to learn how to manage others, putting more care into the skills of communication and persuasion than they think necessary. When working with other people, the 'rules of engagement' should change. A common language for thought makes people able to recognize when thinking changes during a project—and better still <u>how</u> it should!

3. What must innovators do?

They act as midwives for the new baby. They must get the new idea adopted, which means evaluating the kinds of communication required and selling it in to those who matter for its adoption and of course to those who will benefit from using it. They make the case for it, by proving first that it works and second that it meets a good purpose better than anything else. Innovators also have to work well with the idea originator(s) so as to get the best out of them in meeting what the 'market' likes. They smooth the path to collaboration, both ways. So innovators must know what is in the real interest of those they seek to convince, and have ready answers to their objections, aware that exceptional ideas are usually too far ahead to provoke enthusiasm, and will also be treated as a risk. Best to go with the grain—without giving up on anything essential to the idea's success.

Good innovators not only see the future but get
others to meet them there.

Not everyone appreciates help when offered and nobody wants an idea if s/he is satisfied with the status quo. The trump card of the innovator is empathy with the potential approver and user—especially as these are rarely in tune! I was lucky when in the 1970s I was chosen by Philips Eindhoven to be their external consultant and join the team set up to research skillful thinking (Denkvaardighede, or DEVA for short). They faced formidable competition to their global position in electronics from Japan: the priority was therefore to champion their key role in the electronics industry by raising the thinking performance of the company's personnel worldwide. The results of this joint development project were achieved over four years and have been implemented ever since in Philips, especially in Research & Development, where there were some 15,000 engineers and scientists. In 2011, the Intelligent Communities Forum declared Eindhoven as the top region in the world: if only I could claim some small connection!

Invention is only the beginning of Innovation…

I have been developing what we learned through continuous action research in many leading companies. On founding The Centre for Effective Intelligence, I have built a network of coaches and consultants, trained and accredited to spread this unique knowhow as widely as possible.

I Wonder is the third of a trilogy of books I have published to give more people access to the fruits of my ongoing research over the past 40 years or so. The first two are *The Colours of Your Mind* (Collins 1987) and *Conceptual Toolmaking* (Blackwell 1991) Innovation itself will be found in my next book and the growing population of users in businesses around the world is now being joined by ordinary families in ordinary homes, through social media and online fun learning from http://www.thunkies.com.

So what can you do if on reading this book you feel the need to discover more about innovation? Perhaps you would like to get ahead of the crowd, speed up your promotion, help other people or just live life better. Why not be in touch with the author email jerry@effectiveintelligence.com or explore the business site at http://www.effectiveintelligence.com/more. The Information Age advances faster and faster; robots are being designed that can actually do more of the work, even of knowledge workers and managers; access to potential information is so prodigious through Google et al.; school education is struggling to be relevant, even when not boring it puts its victims off learning for life. All these present a clear priority for embracing sound processes of thought, so that you know what data you need to search for and how to use it to really <u>inform </u>your decisions.

4. Should we model thought?

In this book the presence of some kind of model of how people think must have shown through in every chapter, though the focus has been mainly on how to exploit the urge to wonder and create new thoughts with ingenuity and imagination. Our mind is surely of such complexity that we just have to bring its workings into some simpler form, so as to recognize what we are doing with it, and how to aim and steer it better.

To speak of direction and control of your own brain leads on to intention, the goal you are trying to reach as you think. Ordinary intentions are about action, what you mean to do. A thinking-intention is about thought, the kind of thinking process to use before you act: it operates at a less conscious level, tacitly. Most of us have only a very blurry notion, from moment to moment, of deep thinking intention, and this accounts for how often we reach the wrong conclusions and do the wrong thing. Now our research since the 1970s has yielded a workable model of mind, based on the discovery and explanation of a whole alphabet of thought. These 25 'thinking-intentions' in various combinations join together to produce everything we aim for with our thinking. Even small children build a wide variety of artifacts from Lego bricks, and the earlier Meccano has been the basis for an even greater range of engineering marvels, often leading their creators to a career. Of course, each of these 25 has many sub-components and the pathways between them are, like the stars, more than we can count. But it is these 'thinking-intentions' that show the way to understanding what different results you get when you wonder than when you come to judgment about what you wondered! You have used different patterns of thought.

The 25 *thinking-intentions* may form into different shapes, reflecting different aspects of the same model of mind. Here we showed the mind divided into Reason, Feeling and Wonder; how things work, why things matter and what else to explore? In my other books these are shown as divided into Judging what is right, Describing what is true and Realizing what is new. In both cases Hard or Cool thought is separated from Soft or Warm. These are very high-level or simple aspects of the model, and at more of a precision level, thinking-intentions reflect and form many different clusters and sequences. They represent the fundamental engineering of thought.

This 'language' for learning applies in three ways. First, to reflect someone's thinking style or approach, through the *Rhodes' Thinking-Intentions Profile*. It has given us a unique and extensive database of the thinking styles of many nationalities, industries, jobs and individuals around the world. So it is possible to find out how you compare your own preferences for tackling difficult situations with the people that surround you and that you deal with. Nowhere else can you get this specific information that's so useful for work and (family) life. Second, to reveal the kinds of thinking required for different kinds of 'task,' such as making choices, developing a plan of action, finding out how something went wrong. Third, to make sure to recognize which of your thinking-intentions would match up to the needs of the task you are facing. This awareness is shown to raise performance all round— giving people the chance to do the best they are capable of. That is the goal of effective intelligence, choosing the right kind of thought for each task and then getting it actually done.

Be aware: all that you do brings about who you become.

5. So what will you do now?
If you have got this far, you may want to find out more from other sources, or to get started right away to put some of these ideas into action. Of course,

you could decide to wait a while until you meet a situation that really needs you to muster all the creative imagination you have. This notion is easy to understand, but not to recommend: don't let the best be the enemy of the good. Even if it takes time to master whatever you have appreciated here, give it a chance to bring you some reward as soon as you possibly can, in spite of perhaps not feeling enough confidence. 'Use it or lose it' is a threat you don't deserve, now you are here. Instead, each time you achieve even a modest success, you grow both your skill and your motivation.

Ideas not followed by action achieve little, and even good intentions dribble away into the sand. People find it's a good tactic to share what they found useful with someone else, or even make a modest, informal presentation to colleagues. The best way to learn something new is to share it with others. This has been done a good deal within our client organizations, and some-times done so well that the company takes it on officially as a program for organizational development. To find out about our family of accredited Associates, please visit http://www.effectiveintelligence.com/contact-us.

But this book has been for you as an individual person, with a private life, friends, and family. Thinking with imagination is just as useful at home as at work or even for serious play. I do hope that the effort you have put into read-ing all this has already begun to release even more of your sense of wonder and imagination.

All that is necessary for the triumph of evil
is that good men do nothing.
EDMUND BURKE, 1729–1797

About the author

An Oxford graduate, Jerry Rhodes has enjoyed three phases in his career: schoolmaster, management and consultancy. Polio robbed him of the first, he rose to be managing director in the second and third he founded his own international consulting practice. His whole life has been engaged in bringing in things new. In education he created a new paradigm for athletics where everyone had his own personal standard to compete against; this brought about continuous rise in performance throughout the school and a record-breaking win in the All-England Schools Championship. In business he was responsible for several major innovations, and joint development with his clients has created a leading edge methodology for successful action, known as Effective Intelligence.

I Wonder joins *The Colours of Your Mind* and *Conceptual Toolmaking* in his efforts to throw light upon and simplify how anyone can make their minds work better for good.

Several of the illustrations come from unpublished work by Cecil William Rhodes, my father.

Acknowledgements

to
Clients involved in action research for Effective Intelligence

Alcan
Alfa Laval
Allied Dunbar
Allied Irish Banks
American Express, Canada

Amica, Finland
Aston University
Bank of Montreal
Barclays Bank
Bayer
Bell Canada
BBC
Bombardier
BP
British Gas
British Rail
Boeing
Clark's Shoes
City of Toronto
Deloitte
Department of Defense US
Department of Navy US
DFS
Dun & Bradstreet
Dunlop
Exxon
Finland Post
Fortum Oil and Gas

GE
Genentech
General Mills
General Reinsurance
GSK
Hame Business Education Forum
Harvard University
Hoechst
HSBC
Hydro One
IAPA
IBM
ICL
Jollas Institute, Finland
Jutland Technology Institute
Kent County Council
Kimberly-Clark
King Edward VI Grammar School
Lex
Lloyds Bank
Local Government East Midlands
Logica
London Life
Manulife
Mars
Massachusetts Institute of Technology
Maustepalvelu, Finland
Metsä-Serla
Michener Institute

Ministry of Natural Resources Canada
Motorola
National Coal Board
National Health Service
National Westminster Bank
Nestle
Niagara Credit Union
Nokia
Northern Telecom
Novartis
Odyssey Charter School
Ontario Principals Council
Parker Hannifin
Pfizer
PirkanmaanOsuusKauppa, Finland
Philips
Police College
Roche
Royal Bank of Scotland
Sanofi Aventis
Saudi Aramco
Scandinavian Airlines System
Sefek
Schulich

ScotiaBank
Sears
Shell
Sokos Hotels, Finland
STAKES Finland
Statoil
Stora Billerud, Denmark
Suomalainen Kirjakauppa, Finland
Technical University of Tampere
Texas National Guard
Thorn Lighting
Tim Hortons
Tyco
UBS
Union Gas
University of Capetown
University of Delft
University of Industrial Arts, Finland
University of Ulster
Urals Energy
VTT Finland
Westpak
York University, Canada
Zurich Financial Services

Further reading

Abel, R. *Man is the Measure, NY The FreePress, 1976*

Adair, J. *Great Leaders,* Adair Press, 1980

Adams, J. *Conceptual Blockbusting,* Freeman, 1974

Amabile, T. M. *Creativity in Context,* Boulder 1996

Agyle, M. *Psychology of Social Situations,* Pergamon Press

Ayer, A. J. Language, Truth and Logic 1934

Ball, P. *Elegant Solutions,* Royal Society of Chemistry, 2005

Barron F. *Creativity & Personal Freedom,* van Nostrand, 1968

Beer J. *Coleridge's Poetic Intelligence,* Macmillan

Belbin, R. M. *Management Teams,* Heinemann 1981

Bernstein, P. *Against the Gods,* Wiley, 1982

Blackmore, S. *The Meme Machine,* Oxford University Press, 1999

Bruner, J. *The Conditions of Creative Thinking,* University of Colorado, 1971

Burke, J. *Connections,* Macmillan, 1978.

Cairns-Smith, A. G. *Involving the Mind,* Cambridge University Press, 1996

Calvin, W. *How Brains Think,* Basic Books, 1996

Capra, F. *Uncommon Wisdom,* Rider, 1988

Chomsky, A. N. Structure of Language, 1962

Collingwood, R. G. *The Principles of Art,* Oxford University Press, 1958

Critchley, K. *Order in Space, Thames & Hudson*

de Bono, E. *Lateral Thinking in Management,* McGraw-Hill, 1971

Dienes, Z. P. & Golding, W. *Learning, Logic, Logical Games,* ESA, 1966

Duncan, R. A. *Architecture of a New Era,* Denis Archer, 1933

Edelman, G. & Tononi, G. *A Universe of Consciousness,* Penguin, 2000

Fabun, D. *Three Roads to Awareness,* Kaiser Aluminium Corporation, 1970

Feynman, R. *Don't You Have Time to Think,* Penguin 2005

Feynman, R. *The Pleasure of Finding Things Out,* Penguin, 1999

Fisher, R. & Ury, W. *Getting to Yes, Hutchinson 1982*

Foster, R. *Innovation, the Attacker's Advantage,* Macmillan,1986

Galton, F. *Hereditary Genius,* Macmillan   1869

Gardner, H. *Creating Minds,* Basic Books, 1993

Garratt, R. *The Learning Organization: the need for directors who think*, Fontana, 1987

Gleick, J. Chaos: *Making a New Science,* Heinemann, 1988

Goleman, D. *Emotional Intelligence,* Bloomsbury, 1996

Gordon, W. J. Synectics, Harper & Row, 1961

Grayling, A. C. *Thinking of Answers,* Bloomsbury, 2010

Greenfield, S. *The Human Brain,* Widenfeld and Nicolson, 1997

Gregory, R. *The Oxford Companion to the Mind,* Oxford University Press, 1987

Guilford, J. *The Nature of Human Intelligence,* McGraw-Hill, 1967

Guion, R. M. *Personal Testing,* McGraw-Hill, 1965

Hanika, F. *New Thinking in Management,* Hutchinson,1965

Harre, H. Rom. *The philosophies of Science,* Oxford University Press, 1972

Harris, T. *I'm OK You're OK,* Avon, 1955

Hochschild, A. R. *The Managed Heart,* University of California Press, 1983

Hudson, L. *Contrary Imaginations,* Methuen, 1966

Hughes, P. & Brecht, *G. Vicious Circles and Infinity,* Penguin, 1975

James, W. *The Principles of Psychology, (1890)* Dover Publications, 1950

Jastrow, R. *The Enchanted Loom*: *Mind in the Universe,* Simon & Schuster, 1983

Jung, C. J. & Storr, A. ed *The Essential Jung,* Princeton University Press, 1983

Kalthoff, O. & Nonaka, I. & Nueno, P. Light and Shadow, Capstone, 1997

Kepes, G. Sign, *Image and Symbol,* Studio Vista Ltd, 1966

Kepner, C. & Tregoe, B. *The New Rational Manager,* Princeton Research Press, 1981

Koestler, A. *The Act of Creation,* Hutchinson,1964

Kuhn, T. S. The Structure of Scientific Revolutios, University of Chicago Press, 1962

Lanners, E. Illusions, Thames & Hudson, 1978

Magee, B. *The Great Philosophers,* BBC Books ,1987

Majaro, S. *The Creative Gap,* Longman, 1988

Maslow, A. *Toward a Psychology of Being,* van Nostrand*, 1968*

Matchett, E. *Creative Action,* Turnstone Press, 1975

McKinnon, D. W. *Personality & the Realisation of Creative Potential ,* American Psychologist, 1965

Midgley, M. *Wisdom, Information and Wonder: What Is Knowledge For?* Routledge, 198

Morris, D. *Manwatching,* Jonathan Cape, 1977

Nayak, P. & Ketteringham, J. *Breakthroughs,* Mercury Books, 1987

Nonaka, S. & Takeuchi, N. *The Knowledge Creating Company,* Oxford University Press, 1995

Osborn, A. *Applied Imagination,* Scribner's, 1963

Parnes, S. *Creativity: Unlocking Human Potential,* Creative Education Foundation, 1972

Paturi, F. *Nature, Mother of Invention,* Thames and Hudson, 1976

Penrose, R. *The Emperor's New Mind,* Oxford University Press, 1989

Piaget, J. *The Language & Thought of the Child,* Routledge, 1926

Pinker, S. *The Language Instinct,* Penguin, 1994

Pirsig, R. *Zen and the Art of Motorcycle Maintenance,* Bodley Head 1974

Polanyi, M. *The Tacit Dimension,* Routledge & Kegan Paul, 1973

Potter, S. *Lifemanship,* Hart-Davis, 1952

Rhodes, J. & Thame, S. *The Colours of Your Mind,* Collins, 1988

Rhodes, J. *Conceptual Toolmaking,* Blackwell, 1991

Rogers, C. R. *Toward a Theory of Creativity,* ETV, 1954

Rose, S. *The Making of Memory,* Bantam, 1992

Russell, P. *The Brain Book,* Routledge & Kegan Paul, 1979

Schiffman, H. R. *Sensation and Perception,* Wiley, 1976

Scruton, R. *Spinoza,* Phoenix, 1998

Senge, P. *The Fifth Dimension,* Doubleday, 1990

Sheldrake, R. Chaos, *Creativity and Cosmic Consciousness,* Park Street, 1992

Simonton, D. K. Scientific Genius: a psychology of Science, Harvard University Press, 1988

Singer, J. L. *Daydreaming and Fantasy,* Allen & Unwin, 1977

Spielberg, N. & Anderson, B. *Seven Ideas that Shook the Universe,* Whiley, 1987

Stenhouse, D. *The Evolution of Intelligence,* Allen & Unwin, 1974

Sternberg, R. J. *The Triarchic Mind,* Vikking, 1988

Stevens, P. S. *Patterns in Nature,* Penguin

Toffler, A. *Future Shock,* Random House, 1970

Van der Venn, C. *Space in Architecture,* Amsterdam 1978

Vroom, V. and Yetton, P. *Leadership and Decision-making,* University of Pittsburgh Press, 1973

Warnock, M. *Imagination,* Faber and Faber, 1976

Wallach, M. & Kogan, N. *Modes of Thinking in Young Children,* Holt, Rinehart & Winston, 1965

Whitfield, P. O. *Creativity and Industry,* Penguin Books, 1975

Wolpert, L. *The Unnatural Nature of Science,* Faber and Faber,1992

Yates, F. *The Art of Memory,* Routledge & Kegan Paul, 1966

Zajonc, A. *Catching the Light,* Oxford University Press, 1993

CPSIA information can be obtained
at www.ICGtesting.com
Printed in the USA
LVOW05s1342090317
526676LV00021B/230/P